FINDI...
ANSWERS YOU
SEEK

FINDING THE ANSWERS YOU SEEK

Wisdom from a Shaman

Joseph White Wolf

LEON SMITH
PUBLISHING

ISBN: 978-1-945446-69-6

Every man is so much more than just himself. He's a unique and amazing expression of a million different things that intersected to create his life. Isn't it a beautiful thing that the same God that made the oceans, the mountains, and the stars thought the world could use someone like you? That is why every person's story is eternal and sacred.

PRAISE FOR JOSEPH WHITE WOLF

Joseph has a sincere connection with nature and its creator. He has a genuine affection, appreciation, and understanding of the invisible force that unites all energies as one and the ability to humbly share his unique perspectives. He does so with a joyful passion that is both honest and accessible. In short, he IS a modern-day shaman.
—Jerry Gilden, Founder of Sedona Ceremony and owner of SedonaVacationVillas.com

Joseph White Wolf, a clairvoyant from a young age, has been traveling with spirits all his life. As a shaman, he heals, transforms, and inspires the lives of people around the world with his pure light. He now shares his lifelong wisdom in his book, which like Joseph himself appears simple, yet is very profound.
—Kristina Paley, Medical Doctor and Healer

I have had the pleasure of receiving spiritual guidance from Joseph. Years later, I still use his insights in my personal life and am grateful the Universe brought us together.
— Mark Keyes, Retired State Police Detective, Director of the Pennsylvania Paranormal Association, *Ghost Hunters* TV show

I have been in the health and spirituality field for forty-six years. I have had the opportunity to be with Joseph as he took me on a quest over the sacred land in Sedona. Joseph's wisdom, demeanor, and heart surrounded our every step and conversation. Truly a man who walks the talk.
—Steven A. Ross, PhD, President, World Research Foundation

Joseph White Wolf is truly connected to Spirit. My wife and I comfortably and easily traveled with Joseph into spirit realms in Sedona.

—Ron Holman PhD, CEO of the Holman Group

I first met Joseph White Wolf while filming top healers and Shamans in 2012. Joseph stood out from the pack. In 2016, he did a healing for my birthday, and once again he blew me away.

—Ken Sheetz, Filmmaker

Joseph has the ability to share knowledge from his heart and soul. With his wisdom, you learn how to raise the level of your vibration.

—Effie Rice, Spiritual Teacher and Ron Rice, Robotics Engineer

Joseph is an authentic and kind shaman, deeply connected with the earth and stars. His wisdom and guidance are as unique as his character, just as uplifting, just as profoundly inspirational.

—Eliza White Buffalo, Spiritual Teacher and Author of *Two Roads Trilogy*

Joseph teaches by opening the door and taking you with him to this more colorful world where respect and love for everything are dominating.

—Margret Völker, TV and Movie Actress

TABLE OF CONTENTS

Acknowledgments   13
Foreword   15
Introduction   19

SECTION 1

Messages From Nature   25
   Sedona   25
   Vortexes   28
   Flowers   30
   Trees   32
   Water   36
   Birds   37
   Animals   40
   Bugs   42
   Rocks   44

Human Nature   45
   Life Purpose   45
   Kachina Doll   48
   Reconnecting   51
   Natural Gifts   52
   Legacy   54
   Givers And Receivers   55
   Healing Gifts   57
   Sharing Gifts   60
   Love Thermometer   62
   Self-Love   64

Resistance   65
Relationships   68
Addiction   69
Outgrowing People   71
Island Faith   75
Entertain Goodness   76
Old Wounds   77
External And Internal Feelers   80
Energized Prayers   82
Faith   84
Loneliness   86
Loving Everyone   87

SECTION 2

Release Processes And Ceremonies   91
    Letters To The Moon And Back   91
    Love Letters To Yourself   93
    Letting Go Ceremony   96
    The Pinecone Process   98
    Shoe Reminders   100
    Lighten Your Heart With A Feather   100
    Growing Self-Love   101
    Ancestral Coin System   103
    Numerology   107

SECTION 3

Blessings For Your Day   111

   True Purpose   111

   Two Ravens   111

   The Eight Ball   112

   Reach For The Sky But Stay Grounded   113

   Let Life Live Through You   113

   Listening Is The Best Medicine   114

   The Four-Legged Shaman   114

   Silent Night   115

   Thanks Mom, For Being You   115

   Take A Peek Through The Keyhole   116

   Listen To The Children   116

   The Magical Moon   117

   Learn From Within   118

   Simple Things Are Important   118

   Sacred Places   119

   Skeptics Are The Best Students   119

   What Makes You Happy?   120

   Let Pain Compensate You   121

   Moving Forward   121

   Flat Land Thinking   122

   Call Someone Today   122

   Lifelong Learning   123

   Everyone Has Unique Gifts   123

   Sunday Is Sacred   124

   Cheers, Mom!   125

   Listen To The Wind   126

   Let Life Live Through You   126

   The Ocean   126

Inside, You're Still An Innocent Child   127
Plan Things To Look Forward To   127
Be Honest With Yourself   127
One Good Thought At A Time   128
Be Open To Learning   129

Conclusion   131
Let's Connect   133
About The Author   135

ACKNOWLEDGMENTS

I want to thank my wife, Leanne, for her love and support through this process. She is the glue that holds my world together.

Thanks to my editor, Maryellen, and all the folks at Leon Smith Publishing for bringing this book to your hands. They made this process painless, and I am forever grateful.

Thank you to all the beautiful souls who have come to work with me in Sedona on the land and have supported the work I do by booking retreats and land journeys.

FOREWORD

I met Joseph White Wolf through an interesting sequence of events. In retrospect, the way things happened seems like a perfect example of what it means to be *in alignment* with like-minded people. Since I had absolutely no expectations from anyone involved, eventually meeting Joseph in person was absolutely magical.

In September of 2018, I was in Sedona with a well-respected spiritual teacher and a small group of people who had spent the past year in a deeply transformative program with her. Someone I didn't know personally saw a photo I posted of Sedona on Facebook and sent me a message. She said she wanted to go on "an authentic shamanic journey" in Sedona before she headed back to Australia. *Could I recommend someone to her?* I had no clue what a shamanic journey was or why she would qualify with "authentic."

I saw my teacher's husband in the hotel restaurant. I asked him if he knew what an "authentic shamanic journey" was and did he know anyone. With a dismissive hand gesture, he said: "Ahhh, everyone and his brother in Sedona is a shaman." (I had no idea what that meant either.) Then, he called out to his wife who was at the other end of the table: "Does Joseph still live here? Do you have his number?" She said she didn't think she had his number but to find him online. Without looking up from what she was doing she added: "He's the only person we'd recommend." Okay, this was easy; there was only one option, so I messaged the Australian woman on Facebook and sent her a link to Joseph's site.

A few weeks later I got another message thanking me for the referral to Joseph. She went on to say that her time with Joseph was an amazing experience. It wasn't what she expected from a shamanic journey, but she was still feeling the transformative, healing effects from it. She seemed especially happy that she was still experiencing releases weeks after she had met him. And she was in awe of the fact that he likely had no idea *how much* of an effect he had on her life.

Thanksgiving weekend, one of my book-writing students I had met through the same spiritual teacher in February of 2009 sent me a text. She said she had referred me to someone who needed help writing a book. His name was Joseph White Wolf.

Hey, I know who that guy is!

Joseph's wife, Leanne, called me soon afterward and scheduled a session for me with Joseph so I could experience his work firsthand. Shortly before Christmas, I met Joseph in Sedona.

There wasn't any small talk. Joseph said he liked to teach using stories. Then, he started talking about a conversation he had with a flower. This was simultaneously jarring and compelling. I had never spoken with a flower or even thought about having a direct conversation with one.

We went out into the red rocks, and I listened to Joseph talk about trees, rocks, energy, and all the messages that we were getting from the world around us. It was like every bird, flower, and tree branch had a little flashlight and was trying to get our attention.

Two things struck me from that first meeting. First, Joseph's face changed dramatically between the time when we started our trek to when we came back. If you had showed me before and after pictures and asked me if it was the same person, I probably would have guessed I was looking at two siblings. The most sense I could make out of this phenomenon is that he becomes filled with Spirit before he goes out with his clients. Then, sharing his wisdom is like a giant exhale.

Secondly, you can feel Joseph's profound love for his mother when you're with him. The way he has translated his grief to be a practical and useful part of his everyday life is both unusual and impressive. Most of us try to bury our grief so we don't feel it. Joseph embraces grief as a different way of experiencing love. He says that if you didn't care about someone, when they passed over, you wouldn't feel anything. If you love someone and they pass over, you're experiencing love in a different way. Of course, he misses his mom, but he has had the courage to embrace grief rather than defaulting to the numbness that most of us create for ourselves. He embraces signs that his mom is always with him and he teaches people how to have confidence in their own signs.

Whether you're going through a deep personal transformation or simply wanting more insights into your everyday challenges, Joseph can help you. Being with him is kind of like spending time with a kid who says things that are so profound, they make you stop and ask yourself: *Why didn't I think of that?* And in those moments of the simple realizations, it's like *you* can finally exhale, only you didn't realize that you were holding your breath in the first place.

For the people who have spent time with Joseph, this book is a way for them to recapture some of his teachings. For people who haven't met Joseph, this book is a way to experience what it's like to sit with him on a rock and just listen. And for generations to come, this book is a legacy of the rich tradition of teaching through storytelling.

The invisible experiences around you are constantly redirecting you to an undeniable inner truth. Be open to receiving all the messages pointing to beauty and goodness that life has to offer. Joseph teaches how to *let life live through you.*

Maryellen Smith
—Writer/Author

INTRODUCTION

Every person on this earth is trying to make some sense of their life. They're on a journey to find their true self. Most times, the journey is difficult. Why is it that the person who is most qualified to understand their own inner-self feels doubt and confusion?

Most all of us latch on to the past that we can't change or live with fear of what's going to happen in the future. Modern life causes us to take detours and get distracted when we're on the path to our own self-discovery. Sometimes it seems like hitting a dead end. There's nowhere to go.

Truth is, even though you feel like you lost yourself, you have an internal guidance system that you can tap into. A shaman's role is to help you make a reconnection between your inner world and outer world. A shaman helps you have faith and confidence that you really *do* know where you are.

If you start researching what a shaman does, you'll find every possible thing you can think of from ancient times until now. There's not one description that fits everybody. The common thread that you would notice is that shamanism is a *way of being* or *a calling* more than a professional title. Even though a shaman might have a following, a shaman is the opposite of a guru or someone who seeks followers. The same way an artist or writer can't be anything other than who they are, a shaman is someone who naturally connects with animals, nature, and the spiritual world. A shaman walks alongside the people in their community, using spiritual energy to help them overcome fears, get balanced, and to reawaken lost and hidden parts of themselves.

Whether you ever meet with or work with a shaman personally, this book is meant to give you some practical wisdom for everyday life. Imagine yourself sitting on a big rock in Sedona with me. The topic you're reading about is what I would say if you asked me a question about it.

You can read the book cover to cover, open it up, and read something on a particular topic, or get a boost to your day with one of my Blessings—my personal perspective on this life and the life beyond. The second part is made up of easy-to-follow processes and ceremonies. You can use them to heal or release things that are holding you back.

Shamans practice noticing and making sense of signs from plants, animals, insects, rocks — everything in the natural world. Like anyone else who works at their craft, shamans are always learning more and more, adding to their understanding of the world around them. Even though you might have no ambitions or plans to become a shaman, you can still benefit by learning from one.

The main ingredient in the shamanic process is confidence. Confidence in knowing your inner truth. That may sound easy, but looking within yourself based on what's being reflected back to you takes a lot of courage. When you're willing to admit what's behind your emotions, upsets, and the things that hold you back, that's true freedom. There's a big difference between carrying around the weight of the world inside you and being aware of the world, as an observer, letting things flow by.

Take a chance on learning more about your inner self. Then, wherever you are will feel like home. And that's when you can make your dreams come true.

From my little patch of heaven in Sedona I say to you, *shamaste*.

The shaman in me sees the shaman in you.

SECTION 1

PART A

MESSAGES FROM NATURE

SEDONA

Years ago, I was back home in northern Ontario, Canada. I was following my path in life and going through some years of deep, deep, inner discovery. I wanted to find out more about myself.

There was a fellow I knew in town. One day I went over and asked him if there were any traditional Native American people living up on the reservation. I wanted to go to one of their ceremonies and find out what types of things were going on. He wasn't too sure what I was talking about. I said, "Well, you know, people who live a spiritual life." He said he'd ask around.

Well, I got a phone call that he set things up, and I got invited to go to a ceremony. It was one of the most beautiful experiences of my life.

Keep in mind that I'm not full-blooded, I have Algonquin blood that came from my grandmother. She was full-blooded Algonquin. My grandfather came over from Ireland, so there was the Irish part. I'm proud to be Irish and Native American.

My father was a fur trapper and with us living that isolated style of life, we really didn't know that we were Native American. Back then, so much stuff wasn't talked about. But, there was a search in me. When we did find out there was some Indian blood in us, it was a great honor. It was a great blessing and it satisfied a few things inside me.

Once I got the phone call to go to the ceremony, everything changed. When I showed up, the chief was sitting there, the lodge master. He waved me over and he looked at me and he said, "I'd recognize you anywhere."

I asked him how he knew me. He said he knew my cousin Bernie. He went to school with him. He said that Bernie's mom and dad took him in just like he was their own. He even called them Mom and Dad. He said, "You're welcome here. You can come and do whatever you like." And gosh, it was such a beautiful thing to be accepted that way.

When it came time for the ceremony part, I got called out with a few others. Everybody left the campsite, and we were to go and sit back in the bush for four days and four nights. And so, while I was sitting out there one day, all of the sudden I woke up, and I saw a vision. It was about the size of the iMax theater. All I could see were red rock mountains.

I looked up and I realized there was somebody sitting on the mountain. I looked closer. It was me! I shape-shifted into the vision, and I saw things in a different way than through my eyes. Red rock mountains, that's all, there were no buildings or anything like that. I thought it was Mars or a different planet. I didn't think there were red rocks on this planet.

I noticed the trees were very green and yet very short. The vision was over but my feelings kicked in. Gosh, it was strong. My feelings, my emotions were there; everything was strong. After my time was up, the lodge master, he tracked me down, followed my footsteps through the bush. And he found me. He said, "Come on, let's go back." On the way back, we talked. Once we got to the, to the longhouse teepee, I looked inside and I saw a man sitting in the corner. I thought, *Gosh, that guy's probably over a hundred years old.*

I wanted to talk to him because I knew he was full of wisdom. I sat beside him and he didn't talk. I asked him some questions and he didn't respond. Out of nowhere, he looked at me and said, "You need to go to Thunder Mountain."

I asked him where it was. No answer. After a few moments, I tapped him on the shoulder and I said, "Is it nice there?" No response. After everything wrapped up, I went home. My feelings were overwhelming.

I started the process. I told everybody to come over and said they could have whatever they wanted. I started giving stuff away, slowly working things down. It was time to go, but where? *Thunder Mountain, where are you?*

I looked on the computer, and I saw a few different pictures of mountains around the world. I saw that one was in Sedona, Arizona. And I said, "Oh, look at those red rocks. That's exactly what I saw in my vision!" And so, the vision, I followed it.

When I came into the community, I felt that I was loved, appreciated, and respected. People were interested in what I had to say, and I didn't feel like myself anymore. I felt important, and it was such a beautiful experience for me. Sedona is a spiritual community. There are no factories and things like that. It's more of a retirement community, but it definitely has a way of calling people into its presence. So, I got here, followed my vision, and ended up at the doorstep.

The first time I landed in Sedona was in December of 2009. It's such an easy, easy place to fall in love with. That's why there are so many second and third homes here. It only takes an hour to fly from L.A. There's a private airport. All these airplanes that are flying around; a lot of them are personal transportation. Sedona is filled with all kinds of people.

VORTEXES

The energy is strong here in Sedona. They call it the *vortex energy*. The whole community is based on spirituality, so there's a lot of movement here. What happens when people come here, it can be a little too much for them at the time. They're not forced to leave, but inside of them, they just don't want to be here and that's all there is to it.

Sometimes they come back years later and don't want to leave. They fall in love because their hearts are ready. It's all good both ways. If I came to Sedona, and the energy kicked me out, I'd use that as a way to figure out a few things. Sedona wakes you up inside and causes you to want to make some changes. If you don't want to make the changes, then there's a good chance Sedona might kick you out.

The beautiful thing is people come here because they are caring. They want to care for themselves. They're hiking, bicycling, or walking the dogs. Everybody's into good health, eating properly, trying to maintain a good long life. When you have a whole community that's like-minded, a lot of things go on. If you step into that, and you're not on the same frequency, things feel a little unbalanced.

Sometimes when you're walking along the trails people are looking for the vortexes they've heard about. *Where's the vortex?* They think that it's gonna look like a geyser at Yellowstone National Park.

Here's my answer: The vortex energy is everywhere. In some locations, it's a little higher than other spots. You have to take the time to stop and feel it.

Basically, for me it works like this: If I asked you to look across all of the land and capture it in one word, as you started to look, the amount of beauty you're seeing in that moment, you're going to start to feel something. To me, that's what vortex energy is. It's a hug from Mother Earth saying, *Hey, thanks for seeing me and thanks for taking the moment.*

When you look a little deeper into that, you see that the amount of beauty through your eyes and your mind measures the amount of beauty within you.

Sometimes people come here and say it looks like the ocean, underwater, even though it's the desert. Let me explain that. When you sit near the ocean, you feel peace and quiet and calm. Most of the time sitting in Sedona, it's the same kind of feeling, you know. It is; it really is.

When you think about it, we're made up of mostly water, and the rest of us is like the dirt. When you go and sit by the ocean, you're sitting in front of both ingredients that you were created from, water and earth. It's almost like going back in time to your birth. You didn't have any thoughts when you came in here. The thoughts started after your birth. So, here's the way I see it: the closer you step to the ocean, your thoughts disappear. You're sitting in the innocence of your birth or going back, like being born again. There is a great peace coming to Sedona. It's the same feeling as the ocean, but it's the opposite landscape.

I look at Mother Earth as the feminine side and the water as the masculine side. You can't live without the two ingredients.

FLOWERS

Nature has its own language that speaks to me, but anyone can get messages from nature, no matter where they are. When you smell a beautiful flower in nature, or even just look at a flower, there's a feeling that rushes through you. To me, again, it's like Mother Earth saying, *Hey, thanks for taking the moment here.* That's a beautiful hug.

One day I was on a nature walk with my stepson, Justin, who was seven at the time. I noticed a flower all by itself. I bent down and I smelled the flower and the flower started communicating with me, started talking back to me.

Joseph, how old are you?

I'm fifty-five.

Oh, you got a few years left, Joseph. I've only got two weeks left. One of them in bloom.

What do you mean two weeks?

Joseph, I'm a flower. I represent the beauty of creation and right now that I'm in my full bloom, I'm thinking, when does my purpose get fulfilled? If I'm beauty, then I need to be seen. Are the birds flying over or ants crawling on me? Joseph, listen to me. When you came over here and bent down and started breathing on me, I released all the essence of my love, and in that moment, you fulfilled my purpose. I have been seen by you. All of the other flowers are asking, "What's it like?" I got to respond, "It's beautiful." My season is so short that every second is like a month. That was my four-month relationship. Thank you, Joseph.

I realized when I smelled the flower, there was a feeling that came over me, like goosebumps. In that moment, that was the flower hugging me back in appreciation for that moment. So when you look out at nature and you get that feeling coming over you, that's nature's way of saying *Thanks for seeing me this way.*

All of the other flowers were asking that one flower what the experience was like when I was sniffing it. The flower just wanted to have its own moment, to be present and appreciate what was happening without any interruptions. It was like that one flower was saying, *Will you give me a second here? Gosh, I want to appreciate this moment because I'm not going to get it again.* The message that came to me in that moment was beautiful because it was all about appreciating beauty while it's there because tomorrow it might not be there. I only have the moments while they're happening.

We picked the flower and brought it home with some other ones. I said to my little fella:

Remember at recess when you got the soccer ball from that other kid and then got it through the pipes of the net? I remember seeing the smile on your face. It was awesome. Do you remember the look on his face? It was a little different. It was the opposite.

That moment right there, what a beautiful memory. So Justin, these are the things in life that happen, you have memories, all kinds of memories. Some of them are very short, some of them are longer, but if you can just appreciate them while you're having them, life will end up being beautiful.

This is what I was teaching him with the flower. Sometimes, beauty, it just doesn't last long. So, you have to really appreciate it while it's there. The season can be short.

The difference between flowers and trees is that trees are there for hundreds of years. They get to see life in its stillness, where with flowers, it's a short, short season. Flowers represent the absolute beauty of all creation; that's their purpose. A tree gives us oxygen, grounding, and a lot of other things as well as beauty. But flowers are total beauty.

TREES

I remember getting up early every morning and looking at two trees outside. Every single day, all day long, the birds would land on one tree. So, I asked the tree sitting beside it:

Do you ever get jealous?

Why?

Well, because this other tree gets all the attention. All of the birds are always landing on it.

I had an eagle land on me once. And all these chickens, they don't mean anything to me. We don't bother with stuff like that. It's not our concern. We were born the way we are, but the thing is we're stationary. We don't move. We wait for everything to come to us. Even the water, when it starts raining. I'll be thinking, "Gosh, I'm thirsty and it hasn't rained for thirty days." All of a sudden here comes the rain and it's driven by me looking out. Gosh, I hope it stops and soaks in the ground a little bit. I can get a drink. Oh, off it goes, goes right on by. You know, I can't even get a drink of water. I look at you humans and I'm thinking you guys have got it made. You can get up, you can go and get whatever you need, and you get to move around you. You're not stationary. You don't have to wait for anything.

Trees teach us to be grounded. How to find comfort in shade. How to appreciate little birds' nests in tree branches that provide a home.

There's so much going on within the trees. No wonder they don't get jealous and all crazy like humans. It's because they hold hands at their roots, and there's no complaint about it. No complaint at all. They don't have anything to prove. Everything is within their hearts and their souls. It's all deep, deep, deep within.

For us, being grounded like a tree, that's how we love. It doesn't matter what's going on around us. What matters is what's going on inside. That's where nature starts to teach us. If you walk by a tree, and then I asked, *What did you see in that tree?* probably nothing. We have to go back. Then you'd stop and look. You'd see a little spider web there. Then, there would be a string of bugs that looked like an army going up the side of the tree. *Where are they going?* And we can climb trees and see things from a higher place, see things differently.

You can have a special relationship with a tree. Here's what to do. Just find a tree that you're attracted to and start opening up. The first thing you're gonna want to do when you open up a relationship is to bring the tree something it wants. Bring some water to that tree and pour water all around it. Give the tree a little hug and ask, *What's your name?* Walk away, wait, and the name will come. It will come in the silence of the wind. It will come, and you'll have a name for that tree, or maybe you want to simply name the tree. Maybe you want to name the tree after your loved one who has crossed over.

At Christmas time, I named a tree after my mom. I put some Christmas bulbs on it and would sit by the tree, remembering my mom, and infusing the love that I have for my mom in that tree, I have no choice but to experience or to feel the presence of my mom and that tree. So, that tree has taken on a new meaning and a whole different life.

One day I was up at the Amitabha Stupa and Peace Park in Sedona, looking at the carving of Buddha. It's a very big, beautiful, carving from Indonesia. I saw some people doing their prayers and worship in front of it. I walked over and I looked at the carving and I got close enough to ask it:

How does it feel to be carved into a man who represents a culture of faith, a religion, love, and everything else is beautiful in this world? How does it feel as the tree to be carved into that man people visit and pray in front of?

Then I went a little further.

How does it feel to be the tree that was the cross that Jesus hung on?

Look at the life that's in a tree so you can have a relationship with a tree, just like a dog or cat or bird or another person. You're not gonna communicate the same way. And that's okay. If I was deaf, we're going communicate a different way. If I was blind, we're going to communicate in a different way, but we're going to communicate. So when it comes to trees, they sit here giving us oxygen. And without a tree, we don't live. So, to give water to a tree and to give a tree a hug, you don't have to feel anything. You just have to understand and know that you're doing something beautiful. The tree never asked for anything and you don't have any expectation of it. That's what love is. Love doesn't ask for anything.

Trees that aren't in a forest, trees that might be born in a nursery, have a different opportunity in life. For most trees, they're stationary and that's not going to change. So, that's it. Somebody's going to walk into a nursery and see you standing in the midst of all the rest of the trees, pick you, and take you home. You're going to be part of a home.

And then the tree sets up its own family roots. It's got a fresh start in life. It's not just a tree in the forest that will never be seen. Trees in the nursery get pedicures and manicures and watered and tendered and taken care of every day. It's not a bad life when you think about it. From a seed in a nursery, taken care of, then into somebody's home.

And then the trees on the side of the roads, they're giving off oxygen, they've got a hard job. They're like the military on the front line, fighting that exhaust and the fumes and the traffic and the noise, but there they stand. They don't complain. You stopped the car for two seconds under the shade.

It's just stands there. Cools you down for that quick second. Doesn't ask for anything.

So, trees are one of the most beautiful things in creation. Homes are made with them. There's so much that goes on in every tree ring. That's another year of life.

The tree from the greenhouse, I wouldn't say that it's better off than the tree in the forest. It's like the difference between being a full-blooded native and part native. You can still experience the culture, but it's in a slightly different way. A nursery tree has different opportunities. That tree doesn't even know about the possibility to be in a forest and it will never know. The nursery tree, the tree in the forest the tree on the side of the road, they're all beautiful. They're all grounded and have a purpose no matter where they are, just like us as humans.

WATER

Water to me is God in liquid form because there is nothing that can live without water. If I look at a rock and say, *Hey, what's that?* It's a rock and you really can't describe it any differently. Compressed sand. It's a rock. What about water? Rain, hail sleet, steam fog, ice, snow, moisture. Look at all the different ways water can express itself or be seen. Look at all the different ways God can be seen.

Water's God in liquid form. We're made up of it. As you start walking towards water, whether it's a river or the ocean, a lake, it doesn't matter, you get very peaceful and calm. What's going on is that you're heading towards the experience of being born again. You're going back to the moment of the main ingredients you were born with, water and earth.

Those are the two ingredients minus our spirit. That is what we are, water and earth. The closer you get to the water, all of a sudden, your thoughts start to disappear. Just like the day you were born. That was when you first started thinking. So as you go back, it's like going back to a little child where you have no thoughts. You just have peace and quiet sitting by the water. It's so peaceful. It's so quiet. That's why—it's because you're sitting in front of the main ingredient you were created from, water.

God in liquid form, you can't live without water; it's vital. You have to drink the purest water you can find and continue to drink a lot of water.

Water's definitely God in a liquid form.

BIRDS

I'm always cutting my hair as an offering to Mother Earth. I brush my hair, take it outside in the spring and cut it up for the birds. I'll put my hair on a tree branch and wait and watch. The birds will come and take it right to their nest.

When the little chick inside the egg starts pecking and banging on the wall of the egg, he'll finally poke through and take his first breath.

On his second breath, the baby bird will ask:

Mom, what's that smell?

Oh, that's Joseph. He's a human. But listen, when you smell that smell, that's his hair. Fly close to him. He'll say hi. It's like he's one of us, spiritual Joseph.

When you see a bird like an eagle or a hawk, it's easy to think that's a message. But there are birds around you all the time, sometimes swooping down right in front of you. *What does it mean? What kind of bird is it?* Just by swooping by you in a moment, you can draw strength from that bird.

The first thing you do is you look at the direction: north, south, east or west. Then, think about what message is in the direction. *Who do you think about when you think of that direction? What's in that direction? What does north mean to you?* Everyone's going online, looking things up, trusting in everybody else's messages. *What about coming up with your own messages, something you can trust?*

Be still and ask, *What could this mean?* and you'll get a message. You can also just observe the bird, see what it does and where it goes. *Is it a seed-eater? Is it a worm-eater?* Think about its diet. *Is it a vegetarian or a meat-eater?*

When you think about the bird and its life, treat that one bird as if that was your only friend in the world. If that was your only friend in the world and you're on an island, you would know every detail of every little nook and cranny, you would know how many feathers are on that bird. So, study every bird like that and there's your message. It's already in there, but you've got to take time.

It's easier to go on your computer, call someone, or get a reading for your message. *What about having your own reading?* Doing that means taking more responsibility not just listening to everybody else. I call it Island Faith, coming home and trusting in your own intuition and judgment. Becoming your own guide as if you were on an island and had to depend on yourself.

When my mom passed over, I put an orange cheesy cracker on the window ledge. A raven came by and took it. So, I put another one out. The raven came again and took it again. It happened three times. And this was on the second story of the house. The raven kept coming, only he started leaving me things for the cheesy. A piece of red string, a bobby pin, a paper clip. It was a little gift exchange.

What if it's my mom? Oh, my goodness. Maybe it's my mom showing up! I wanted to stall the raven, to get its full attention, so I put out two cheesies, knowing it couldn't take them both at once. After the raven picked up the first cheesy, I said, *Mom is that you?* The raven looked at me with his beady eye against the beautiful, black feathers. I didn't see anything, but I did get my message. When the ravens come now, they come close to catch my attention. I'm not looking for them. It's like they're trying to get my attention. The ones trying to catch my attention are my loved ones, the people who have crossed over. They're coming close saying, *Hey, I'm here with you.* Every time I see a raven, and I wave and say, "Hi Mom."

It's nice. It's comforting. I know my mom's body, soul, spirit is not in that bird. She's left her physical life. But it's the memory, the beautiful memory in that moment, and my mom's with me. I'll take any, any memory I can get because then I'm experiencing love.

When you see bluebirds, they're asking you to take a close look at your love. The bluebird reminds you to make sure you're not giving more than you're receiving. *What does it mean to take a closer look?* Ask yourself, *What am I doing with my love? Am I sharing more than I get in return? Does everyone around me just take, take, take?* The bluebird says, *Put love into balance so everybody learns, everybody grows, and everybody gets to have their own boundaries.* They're good messengers.

If a snake comes in our yard, there will be three of those bluebirds or blue jays that will start chirping away like crazy. If it's only one bird, it's just an alert. But if two of them or more are squawking, that means there's something coming into the yard with four legs, and there's an emergency. So, we watch them, we use them; they're like burglar alarms on our property. It's the coolest thing. My wife is the one who caught onto it. She's the one who recognized if the wild pigs, the *javelinas,* are coming into the yard, the birds let her know. She knew if the wolf was coming in the yard before it got there. She could tell from the sound of those birds. Birds are beautiful messengers.

ANIMALS

All of my animal and bird messages are my own, from my own experiences. Getting animal messages is the same as any other things you see in nature. Basically, there's a message within yourself. If you look at a cloud, and it looks like a head of a white wolf right in the middle, *what does the wolf mean to you?* A wolf is a teacher or a protector. There's a message there, but you can keep looking and interpreting things around it, like other shapes in the clouds. Look for good messages.

The first thing to do is you've got to set up your inter-pretation, and then you see the signs and connections in the world. That makes it so much easier. We can all have our own interpretation chart, we can all have our own graphs and stuff, and we can all interpret our own visions and dreams and get our messages in nature. Just walking and paying close, close, close attention is all you need to do.

Me, I count things. I'm a counter, I remember numbers, and I also have things happen more than once. If something happens twice, three times, you've got to pay attention. I'm always looking for patterns as well. If you sit long enough and study, the message will definitely come. When you write all your messages out, there's your interpretation. You don't really need to ask anyone.

Messages are everywhere in everything. Think about an old log, just sitting out in the woods. It looks like nothing at first, but then you see the shape of a snake in a twisted branch. Once you see it, it changes your view. Then, you can ask, *what's the message here?* Snakes shed about three times a year so that's one message to think about. *What's something that you need to leave in the past, behind you?* It's dangerous to drag the past into the future.

Maybe when you look closer, you see that it's not really even a log but a part of a big root system that's exposed. So when you're looking at it, you can think, *There's something that's exposed that needs to be let go.* It might not be something that anyone else sees, but it can be personal to you. So, you have to think for a second and be honest. *What can it be? What can I learn from it?* That's how it works for me. That's how I do it.

There's going to be a message in everything. The moss on a rock, slowly disintegrating, eating that rock back to sand. It's a slow process. So, there it is, a message of patience. Even litter sitting in nature can have a message. A plastic cup out in the woods looks negative, but a plastic cup on the beach that a little kid is using for a sand castle, that's a tool for creativity. That litter in one situation can be a blessing in another. You have to look past the negative and see the good. Every person can interpret messages from nature within themselves. It all depends on how they use their ability to interpret.

Let's say I was an artist; there's a good chance nature is going to speak to me through color. *What colors do you see? Green, red? Are there different kinds of green?* Other things you can use might be shapes, like the shapes of rocks. There are heart shapes in nature that can speak directly to your heart. Everything depends on how you communicate and how nature communicates with you. And if someone else sees something in nature that you don't see or you see something they don't, so what? How you see and what you see are your own interpretation. Nobody's wrong. Your soul is speaking to you through the message. *What does it mean to you?* You don't have to go online and look things up.

BUGS

When you question your messages or look to other people to see the same thing that you do, you're saying that one person has to be wrong and one has to be right. It doesn't have to be like that. More than one person can be right even if they don't have the same interpretation. You've got to create your own messages and have faith in them.

Let's say you see some bugs on the ground with big wings. *What do those big wings, that are ten times the size of the body, mean?* It could mean you can get somewhere fast.

It could mean you can change where you live easily. It could mean freedom. *Time flies? You're bugging me?* Maybe because there are a lot of bugs scattered around, it means there are a lot of possibilities. One message might feel stronger to me than to you. That doesn't mean your message is wrong if I don't see it your way.

With every footstep you take, nature will talk to you. That's how nature works. And it's kind of like you're asking *What are you trying to show me here?* so that the thoughts will come. Just relax into the thoughts; let them come and go. Even if the thoughts seem bizarre, whatever comes, there will be a message when you write it out, later or in a couple of days. You'll think of the message again and be able to touch it up and add a little more to it. It's like you're writing up a book of your own messages, your own path. It's all there. So then, you start to trust those messages because they work, and they'll prove themselves to you. Allow messages from nature to prove themselves.

Always look for the good in messages. But the interpretation of the sign from nature, that doesn't mean everything is going to happen exactly like you think it is. You have to pay attention and stay open. When you stay open, you have options. And it's nice to have a few options. If you're not open, then the signs you get from nature might seem wrong or bad. You can't blame nature for signs or think that your intuition is wrong if something doesn't happen.

What I'm saying is to learn from the inside out. Start where you are. Most people sit in a classroom, listen to the teacher, take in information, and process it from the outside in. With nature, you have to go deep within yourself and ask what you're feeling inside. *What do you already know?* It's a different way of learning.

When you learn from the outside in, you never feel like you have enough. You always have to be filling the bubble with information, and you keep feeling like you need more and more. More knowledge, more wisdom; you just have to start and let it grow like a muscle. Once you start, things will come to you. Once you start learning from the inside out, you'll be more confident in your own messages. You can't learn everything at once; you just have to start. You'll never become what you want to be unless you start. Surround yourself with people who appreciate you and look for people you can help.

ROCKS

Each rock is like a person and there are different races, skin color, abilities, and gifts. Every rock is unique, the same as a human being. For myself, if I'm walking along and I see a rock, I'll pick it up and say, *Would you like to come home with me?* It's either going to be a yes or no right away. If I take that rock from that location, it represents my trip, the memory of the community, or location. It represents so much more than just sitting there in the ditch.

Some people, they're gonna love a certain type of rock or gem more than another, and it's going to resonate differently. Just like friends. Each rock definitely has its own qualities. It has its own purpose and it has its own healing abilities. It definitely depends on what you resonate with, for sure.

PART B

HUMAN NATURE

LIFE PURPOSE

Life is a beautiful gift. Every day, as soon as you wake up, you open up a new gift. And the gift of life is love. For me, our purpose in life is to love ourselves because we have a global purpose to love each other the same way that we receive love from above from our creator. Once you start to love yourself, you become a greater gift to other people.

When my mom crossed over, I missed her dearly. One day I was sitting outside, and it was almost like she was looking down from the clouds. I had tears in my eyes.

Mom, I miss you.

Listen, you call it grieving; I call it love, Joseph. Every ounce of it is love. The love that you have now or all the love you ever shared with me. Now that I'm on the other side, I can't take it with me. I used the blue jay to show you. I can't take it with me, so I have to return all of the love. So, what I've been doing since I passed over is returning all the love. Every single person who has gone through my life. I've returned the love they shared; it was a gift. The love that you share is the love you have for yourself. You can't share what you don't know and is not yours to share. That's why we try to become more loving, so we have more to share. The love that we have for ourselves is what we share.

My mom said I'd changed so much, and I was a lot more sensitive.

Joseph, oh my God, how am I going to do this? It's like trying to get a camel through the eye of a needle.

The amount of love that you've shared with me . . . it's so much. Here's what we're gonna do. I'm gonna have to send it a little at a time. You're going to be like the space shuttle. You're going to get shaken up and bent out of shape . . . missing me and crying the blues. But you better enjoy those moments of shaken up, because the shaking measures the amount of love you shared.

Joseph, if you didn't love me and you really didn't care, then you wouldn't have a thought or felt all of these feelings and emotions flowing through you. That's your love returning home to be shared again, so enjoy the moments of your grieving because it's actually your healing, and after you're done, you're going to see and experience me in a whole new way.

So, I walked and walked. I saw things and my mom started revealing herself to me. Because she was a professional smoker and a professional drinker, she left a lot of clear messages. One of them was cigarette smoke. She could blow three cigarette rings right through each other. And so, I picked up my first cigarette butt off the ground. I thought, somebody left a cigarette butt, and they probably enjoyed the smoke just as much as my mom.

So, I held it high in the air and I said, "Thank you, thank you for leaving me this beautiful memory of my mom," and I put it in my pocket. I picked up the next one. I thought, *Mom, remember that time I didn't get any Valentine's cards in grade three? We drew those pictures together and you made me feel good. I still to this day remember the crayons and everything.* "Thanks, Mom!" The next cigarette butt, I remembered a few spankings, but I also remembered that those spankings stopped me from doing crazy things. The fourth time I started picking up the butts there was a full-length cigarette. I knew the story. Somebody was in a hurry, they needed to get in the car and the other people didn't want them to smoke. When I went to pick it up, it was like my mom was standing behind me, looking at me.

Joseph, don't pick up that cigarette butt. You don't need it to remember me. I'm right here!

I realized that day that my mom was always by my side. If I was missing my mom, I'm the one who's alive. I needed to show her what I was doing, what kind of memories I was looking for. So when I started picking up cigarette butts and holding them in the air, I could see my mom on the other side . . . she'd get my grandma, my grandpa, my nan, my little sister Mary . . . get them all together and chit-chat it up. Now, looking down, she said, *Look at him; look at him picking up those butts. Now, you want to tell me that I wasn't loved? That's my son and he still loves me.* When I had that feeling coming over me, I knew that was my mom. Her presence doesn't need to go anywhere. I can go anywhere and feel the presence of my mom. And it's such a beautiful gift.

KACHINA DOLL

When you're grieving your lost loved one you need to grieve properly. You shouldn't try to get rid of the memories. Holding the memories makes the connection stronger.

I got a phone call from a man from Mount Shasta. He said:

Listen, I heard about you. I want to come down and see you.

I said, Okay, what's going on?

Well, my wife died.

Oh sir, I'm sorry.

Yeah, well, I really loved her. Joseph. I really, really did. One time we were in Sedona and we bought one of Kachina Indian dolls, from one of the stores there. It's here and I thought, *One day I'm going to go back and I'm going to buy the other version, the female version.* We bought the male and I want to have the girl and the boy one. So, we're together again.

Right away, instantly, my throat choked up. I could feel a lump coming up and I thought, *I'm going to cry right here on the phone.* And I'm not a crier, but I can feel the tears coming. I said, "Sir, you're very sentimental. That story really touches me."

Oh Joseph, you want to know what else happened?

He kept talking. Eight tears came from each of my eyes, so I grabbed a napkin and I saved them.

About five days later, he drove down and made his way to the house.

Are you the Kachina man?

Yes, I am.

Come on in and sit down. We need to talk.

I said, Sir, what are you doing running around the country looking for something? What is all this about?

I said, You know, I think she's resting comfortably and she's at peace with the tombstone.

I said, You're not looking for a tombstone. You're looking for a memory.

I said, Sir, do you have any ashes?

He said, No, they're all gone.

I said, Okay, here's what I'd like to do, if it's okay with you . . . Do you know, when you called me on the phone, you did something to me? You made me cry, sir. Eight tears. I saved them in this napkin. Can we use them as ashes, and we're going to rest their memory?

He started crying, so I gave him the napkin and said, "Add a few more."

We went up the side of a mountain. There's a twisted tree. They call it a *vortex tree*. We took the napkin and we lifted up the rock and we put the napkin underneath.

Now sit on top of all this, put your feet on the ground with her. Sit down and give the tree a hug. What was your wife's name?

Lisa.

Okay. This tree's name is Lisa, and the memory of your wife is resting, and you can give her a hug.

When he put his arms around the tree, his legs came up and he went into fetal position. I took his photo.

Listen, sir, when it gets to be too much, call me up, just call me up. Say, "Joseph, I can't take it anymore. I miss her too much. I want to be able to take that burden. I don't want you take it around." I'll drive up the hill and sit with the tree, and I will tell Lisa how much you love her and how much you miss her.

Then he was standing there looking out at the mountains. "Look at the view she's got!"

As soon as he said, *Look at the view she's got,* I knew that he left the sad memories in the tree. It was over. And we had our beautiful moment.

Now whenever you're sitting, wherever you're sitting, and you start talking with somebody, and they open up in a moment, whether it's in the airport, the bus stop, in the office, the cafeteria at school, I don't care where it is—hiking trail, restaurant, a public washroom—and someone starts crying, pass them a tissue.

After it's over, say, *Listen, in that moment when you were talking, you released a lot of pain and I'm sorry it all happened. I appreciate you trusting me with your story, but what are you going to do with it? Why don't you take that Kleenex now, take it into the woods and burn it and just let it go. Throw it in the river, let it go, flush it down the toilet, but let it go. Do something with it. The answer is in your hand. The pain's already been released in the story. Now let's do something with it.*

My father was visiting. When I dropped him off at the shuttle, on my way back home, I started crying. And I don't cry that often. I went in the house and I grabbed one square off the toilet paper roll. I put it on my face and I patted it lightly and captured the tears. I folded it until it into a small square. I got some red thread and I wrapped it and I made the symbol of a red cross. As soon as you see that little piece of tissue paper, you can see that red cross, the symbol of an emergency. I used it for an emergency because he had to go for a cancer operation. And, if I ever wanted a prayer to be answered, that was it. I used the paper to offer my tears. I'm not taking the credit, but he is fine and I'm glad I had the folded tissue. It was the offering for my prayer.

RECONNECTING

When you lose a family member, especially a child, it's the most difficult thing. There's no greater love in the world than between a mother and a child. The pain is so real and strong. When it comes to stuff like this, when you're really missing someone on a deep level, one of the reasons for that is there are unspoken words. You didn't get to say something you wanted to say, like to tell them how much you love them or miss them or forgive them. What I do is write a letter and mail it back to myself. Or, I write a letter on someone's behalf and mail it. When it gets delivered, I receive it as if it came from the person.

My sister Kimberly's birthday is on Halloween. When we were kids growing up, I always felt that it wasn't fair to have a birthday on Halloween that changed our plans. As an adult, I felt bad about that. It's just a date; it's got nothing to do with her. She's a beautiful soul.

One year on her birthday, I sent her a card. On the back of the birthday card, I wrote my mom's full name, my mom's address—the home we all grew up in, the city, the postal code, and her phone number. Inside the card was a letter I had written, as if it had come from my mom, telling her about the transformation she went through with Kimberly being her first born, how much she missed and loved her.

I just want you to have a wonderful birthday. Happy Birthday. Love, Mom

My sister phoned me when she got the card. She was crying because it touched her heart. She said, "I wasn't expecting to get a birthday card from Mom." At that point, Mom had been gone for ten years. It meant a lot to her read the words that she wanted to hear but thought she could never hear again.

These letters are something you can do in other situations, like when you need to forgive someone. If there is a person who crossed over and that person wasn't good to you, you can write an apology letter from them to you. It would be the apology that you always wanted but never got. Then, you can put your hurt and anger to rest and move beyond it. It doesn't mean what the person did or said was right; it just means that you can put situations behind you.

NATURAL GIFTS

One of the hardest things for me is when people come to me and ask: "What am I supposed to do with my life? What am I doing here? What's my purpose?"

We're all gifted. Every single one of us—we're all gifted in very unique and beautiful ways. You just have to find your gift. The thing is, your gift doesn't make everything in your life magically fall into place all at once. You have to work to use your gifts to help other people. The answers are inside of you. You have to look within.

The things that you've mastered need no attention at all. It's the troubled stuff that constantly asks for attention. You have to think about what you've mastered.

When you see someone you know going through a hard time, and you think, *I'd never in a million years let myself go through that,* there's a sign. If you'd never let yourself go through that situation, then you've mastered what it takes to overcome that problem. So, your gift is to be able to help someone else get through their hardship. Maybe it's giving them a book. Maybe if you're a healer, you can offer them a healing session. Or it might just be a prayer for them, depending on the situation.

The most painful experiences that we go through in life end up being the best teachers.

Life is all about discovering and growing into your gifts because those gifts are who you are. And so, you're becoming yourself, which is the most natural thing in the world. You don't really have to work at it, you were born that way.

The funny thing is, if you have a gift, you assume that everybody else has the same gift and sees, feels, and senses the same thing, but that's not true. We all see everything uniquely. If you don't think that's true, all you've got to do is go to the movie with friends. Then ask everybody what their take was on it was. When you're listening, you'll think you were at a different show because we see and feel things so differently. Your natural gifts tie into your purpose.

LEGACY

You don't really *find* your purpose; you grow into it. Life is a great opportunity. You're like the flower with the purpose to be seen. The memories you leave behind are the way you live on in spirit. Everybody leaves different things behind.

There's a beautiful bronze plaque for a woman named Rachel who bought some property. She refused to build a house on it and left it for everybody to enjoy it. It's the best view in all of Sedona. Every time I go up there and look out, I see the legacy she left behind. I feel like she left it for me and I'm home, even though I never even met her. So, a part of our purpose is to leave memories behind so people remember us. No matter how big or small, regardless of what your situation is, you create memories.

It's important not to waste your time. You could be the most brilliant mind in the world, but if you're addicted to video games, you're not growing into your purpose. But maybe your purpose, mission, or what your soul needs to do has nothing to do with your family. That's fine. Your purpose might be elsewhere, for someone else.

You grow and evolve and outgrow things. You have an individual purpose and a global purpose. *Are you going to live your life, or are you going to let life live through you?* I'd rather let life live through me and accept each footstep one at a time. That way it makes it a little easier on me. Just let life live through me. I can't control it anyway, and actually, the more I tried to control my life, the harder it got. I just let it live through me. That's a wonderful way to live.

When you walk into the wilderness and then come back out, I might ask you, *How many broken branches did you see out there?* You probably didn't notice any. Those broken branches are like all the stuff from your past. Treat your past like you'd treat those broken branches in nature. Just walk by them and leave them behind.

GIVERS AND RECEIVERS

My cop friends would say, "You're lucky! When you show up, everybody's happy to see you. When we show up, everybody runs or starts yelling and calling us names. Nobody really appreciates us, unless there's no problem or crime. Then we're welcomed so differently."

I've thought about this a lot. That's how everybody feels about any career they choose, not 100 percent appreciated for what they do.

There are some careers where you receive and there are some where you give. If I'm a giver, a person who loves to give, then I should be in an occupation where I can satisfy that gift and give all day long. If I'm a receiver, I need to be in a career that allows me to receive so that I can receive all day long, satisfy that gift within me and share it.

Would you say a locksmith is a giver or a receiver? I was a locksmith, a safe cracker — it was both giving and receiving. It was a very satisfying occupation. Not everybody has the gift of sensitivity to do that kind of work. When I touched the safe dial, *it's not what I felt, it's what I didn't feel.* There's a little bit of mystery in how a safe opens up. It's like fishing. You're holding a fishing rod, and you can feel something nibbling down below that you can't see, and that's the same kind of thing in the locksmith trade. It was very satisfying to know how to do something that was a real mystery to others.

I learned how to be a locksmith when the company I was working for went bankrupt. I needed a job. I was young, I was nineteen or twenty, and I had a little girl and a wife. I went out to breakfast and the lady who was serving me said, "You should go over to the locksmith shop. He's an elderly fella and he needs help. He's really busy. He didn't even have time to sharpen a knife for us."

So, I went over and I said, "Hey, I understand you might need a little help."

We talked for a few minutes, and he gave me this great big book of locksmithing and said, "Go home and read this and come back Monday morning. See you at eight o'clock."

And so, I showed up on Monday. He looked at me and said: "Did you read that book?"

I said, "No, I couldn't read that book. I don't even know what they were talking about in there, all these tumblers and stuff."

He grabbed the book, put it back on the shelf, and said, "That's all I wanted to know. If you would've told me you read that book, I'd say, 'You're full of it. Get out of here.' Now I know you're honest."

Then, I watched everything he did, and that's how I learned.

I learn through observation. That's my gift. I watched my dad my whole life doing things, fixing things, and as soon as I saw how he did it, I followed suit and I was able to do the same thing. With observation, you need a strong ability to receive information that you're not hearing. That's what I did when I was a safecracker.

So, what do you do with all that information you receive? Some people might be great at fixing stuff or mechanically inclined. I call it a *gift* because not everybody can do it. If you can do something very easily, and it comes naturally, that's your *gift*. Other people have to study and work hard to do the same thing. When it comes to your gift, you need to acknowledge it and run with it. There are probably a million ways that you can apply your gifts, so you have to be creative about it.

Now, I do spiritual land tours and talk to people about the things they *see* and *don't see* in nature. Do you understand how I'm using the same gift, learning through what I saw being a locksmith?

HEALING GIFTS

If you have a gift to heal, you're born to help people heal in whatever capacity your gift needs to be satisfied. *When you open up and start to help people, does it feel satisfying?* If yes, there's a good chance that the relationships that come your way could be more of a client, rather than a personal friendship. Your gift is actually a hunger, and the law of attraction will bring people into your presence so you can help them. Once you start working your gift, it's like a muscle that gets stronger. Then everything else in your life is different.

I get a tremendous number of healers who come to me and ask me questions. Here's what I ask them:

What is it you want to help people with and how did you learn how to do it?

That's the first thing. *What do you have to offer?*

Most people say, "Well, I don't know. I know I'm gifted, but I really don't know what to do."

I say, "Okay then, the second step is to look at your friends and the people in your life. Think about the people you see on a day-to-day basis. *What are they going through? What do they complain about?* You can see it plain view, but they can't see it. What you're experiencing is something you've mastered. Once you've mastered something, it doesn't ask for your attention. You take it for granted. You might even look down at the person because they don't know what is obvious to you. The truth is you've got something. You've got to figure out how to put what you know into a form of information that other people can understand. *How can you walk in their footsteps and help them understand what you know?*"

The first step is: find out what you've already mastered or healed.

What happened?

How did you heal?

How did you get where you are?

Did it take a long time?

When you understand how you got through your pain or challenges, that's what you can use as a healing session.

When you're at a point where you've been through something very difficult in life, extremely difficult, that not many other people have been through, there's a reason for that. Now you have something that can really help other people with what they're going through. What happens then is that your pain starts to compensate you for what you've been through.

Then in your session, you share what you went through, explain what you did to get over it, and hopefully, it works to help the other person. If not, together you can brainstorm and come up with other ideas that might work even better. It's not important that you didn't go to University to learn what you know or have some kind of certificate. Real-life experience counts when it comes to helping people.

It's hard to put a price sticker on what you're doing, but it's not about the price. It's about being in service to others and allowing your pain to start compensating you. That requires you being able to receive. Allow yourself to feel good about what you've been through, what you've learned and overcome. Once you get booked up, you can raise your prices because you don't live to work. You need some enjoyment. Raising your prices is a way to honor the gift that God gave you. You spent a lot of time learning what you know, probably years. It's okay to get compensated for your time.

Hard work is how you get ahead. It doesn't matter what you're doing. You dedicate yourself to something, work hard, and then you will become successful. It's not something that's going to fall out of the sky for you. You have to decide what success means to you. *Is it money? Is it satisfaction? Is it personal peace?* Figure out what you want and then work hard at it.

SHARING GIFTS

For people who have trouble charging for their services or feel like what they do, *their gift,* comes so naturally they should do it for free, that's not allowing their pain to compensate them. It's just where they're at. I was in exactly in the same spot. I'd think, *Gosh, I can't charge for this. It's like I have a gift and Spirit's working through me.* Then one day, I started looking at other people who use their gifts and get financially rewarded.

The first person I thought of was Muhammad Ali. *When, when did he get beat up? Who punched him first to give him the ability to respond?* Because once he did, his gift opened up, and he knew how to use his fists in that ring and made a very good living. And there are many others who use the same gift. That was their gift. I don't have that gift personally, but if I wanted to learn to box and Muhammad Ali would teach me, that would be worth something. It wouldn't take me as long to learn from him as it would on my own because he had mastered boxing. It would save me time to learn from him.

What about Elvis Presley? He sang it all. He did it all. And to this day, everybody knows who Elvis is. He used his gift to sing and make a living. I don't think Elvis was about to start doing birthday parties for children. It's not that he didn't want to; it's just the demand on that man was to sing for thousands instead of twenty. It's just the way it was; his gift multiplied. And everyone was honored by his gift.

People like Elvis or Muhammad Ali, there's no difference between them and you and me. You can't look at everyone else as more accomplished than you and then think that you're less.

You have to look at yourself, your own cage, your own world that you're living in. You have to work with the tools you have. These days, everything's changed. It's all about marketing. You could have exactly the same gift, the same product, the same everything. And if you're just sitting at home, telling the same old story you've been telling yourself, not sharing your gifts, nothing is going to change. You're going to stay right where you are. Someone with the same gift looks at it, sees that it is valuable, and says, *You know what, I'm going to market this. I'm going to do something with it.* Next thing you know, they're multimillionaires because they did something with that gift.

It's up to you. If you feel you shouldn't ask for money for sharing your spiritual gift, then don't ask for money. That's fine. If you feel you should, allow your gift to compensate you. Then, you're energizing your gift. It's not selfish in a bad way to be able to receive something back when you share your gift. It's a beautiful thing to acknowledge that you have a gift and let it be there to provide you with a very comfortable living that allows you to be in your passion. I don't think there's anything wrong with that at all. Nothing at all.

Spiritual gifts all come from feminine ancestors. They come from Mom, Grandma, Great-grandma. All of the spiritual gifts are tender and loving. They're kind and healing.

People who come to me who are already working as healers usually have two things they're looking for. One is they've taken on a lot of energy from all the people who come to see them. They feel overwhelmed and a little bit burnt out. In that case, we release that energy. That's an energy clearing. Other people are looking for new modalities for healing. So when we walk around the land, and I find out what's going on in their life, we'll make a healing tool out of something we find. Then, they'll take that back with them.

You don't have to be a healer to take on too much energy from the people around you. I've also had musicians who perform in large stadiums that feel tired from having too many people around them. In those cases, we'll do a clearing too, so they'll get their energy back.

LOVE THERMOMETER

Think about love like food. *Are you oversharing with everybody, piling up other people's plates and not keeping any for yourself? Is there more love piled on other people's plates than they could possibly even digest in one sitting?*

Here's what I did. I cleared all the plates off the table in my mind. I reset the table and I only put a little crumb on each plate. I waited to see who was with me for a crumb. The first phone call came from my youngest son. "Dad, I'm in a snowstorm. I'm going to be late for work, but I'm alright. I just wanted to call and tell you I love you. Thank you, Dad." In that moment, he was meeting me where I was at, and I really needed to hear that. He had never done that before, called me during the day.

I realized I'd been putting too much food on everybody's plate. So, I had to reduce it a little bit. Everybody started getting hunger pains and only I could satisfy them. I realized that if you want to be loved, meet everybody where they're at, don't overdo it. Only share the portion of love that the other person is willing to accept from you at that time. That's what it means to meet them where they're at. You're not overloading them. You're not under-loving them. The portion is just right.

When I look back at all my old relationships, I realize in a lot of cases I loved people, but I didn't have anything left for myself. I didn't love myself that much.

Thousands of people have come to see me over the years. I listen very carefully, like it's my classroom. A lot of women come and they say, "You know, Joseph, I've loved him a lot more than he's ever loved me. I've given a lot more than I've ever received."

I look over at them and ask, "How's that working for you?"

They usually say, "He used me," but then I'll repeat, "How's that working for you?" so they can think about what they're saying more deeply. When someone's got my back, I know they really love me, but there needs to be balance in the relationship.

Love is like a thermometer that goes from one to twenty. First, you have to gauge where you're at, figure out what number. That's how I measure it. Every incident is different. I'll ask: What would I do for this person? What would that person do for me? Well, maybe the answer is three, not too much. Then I know my love for them is not that strong. It is what it is, though. With someone else, there's nothing I wouldn't do for them. That person might be a twenty. Well then, I know my love is very strong. And if there's nothing they wouldn't do within their power for me, then I know their love is strong too. The numbers are about the same on both sides.

Love is always at all different levels with people. You have to look at the balance. So when the bluebird comes, that's exactly the message he's bringing you, reminding you of self-love. It's not easy to open up and receive when you're a giver. But when you're out-loving other people, it's because you feel like nothing's coming back to you. Then, it's the opposite of what you expect, you end up turning the other person away. Everybody is where they're at. Don't overdo it with love, giving someone more than they can handle.

You stop overgiving by starting to receive. That's how you do it. You have to set it up though. *If you're overgiving, what's the reason? Why are you giving so much?* If you're giving too much, then your expectation of what you should be receiving is probably unequal. That's a setup for disappointment because other people will not give you as much as you're giving, because you're not paying attention to where they're at.

You want to be loved and appreciated, and you want to be seen. You want other people to care. So, you figure, *If I give love out, maybe it will come back to me the way I want it to.* What I realized when I was overgiving my love is that I was throwing my love out like a handful of seeds, hoping something might stick and grow. I stopped and looked at the value of my love. I decided to plant my seeds and water them to make sure they were doing exactly what they were intended to do. And then I wasn't giving as much, scattering my love all over the place. I see it as loving thoughtfully.

SELF-LOVE

There is this kind of global love, love for all humans and the people around us. Love has a lot of dimensions. If you're loving yourself to your fullest, then you have that to share with the rest of the world. It's not like you're searching for it, trying to bring it in. It's there and it just beams out from you. When you want to be in a relationship and you stop looking and obsessing on it, that's when it happens.

Sometimes when you wake up, you're in a little slump. Set up the day, write a few things down, and tell a happy story. Then, put something in your shoe, like a penny. Every time it rolls around remind yourself, *I'm a good soul; I love myself.* It's a constant reminder all day long, and the more you put happy thoughts into your mind, the more negative thoughts you're getting out. If you control your mind, that's the key to happiness. It's all in the mind in the first place. Every single thing that goes on, it all starts in the mind. You can control your thoughts.

You can't have two thoughts going at the same time. You can't look at a rock and be thinking about the rock next to it. You can bounce back and forth fast. When an unhappy thought comes, you stop it at the door. Then the thought backs off and won't weigh you down. Don't entertain the unhappy thought. Then the thought gets weaker and weaker and you get stronger and stronger. It becomes almost like a cartoon. It's a little movie of how you overcame something. What are you thinking that you need to break away from?

RESISTANCE

When I realized I wasn't controlling my mind, that's when I knew how weak I was. I thought I was strong. My mind was tricking me. Once I figured out my thought processes, everything changed.

I was in a very serious accident, suffered a brain injury, and lost sight in one eye. Man, I went through a lot. I pretended I was okay and everything was fine until one day, I snapped. I just couldn't take the anger I had inside and I blew up. I look back and I can see what happened. Sometimes it's like you're a balloon getting overfilled with air and it pops. As a result of all that, once I kind of exploded, everybody started asking me a lot of questions because they had never seen me act that way. I was getting a lot of attention and I enjoyed it.

People were coming up to me, talking about feeling sorry for me, telling me that they wished it didn't happen. I kind of fed into it, and I felt pretty good, getting so much attention. I got sucked into my emotions and my feelings and sucked in to babying myself with the attention. I told everybody about my pain. One day I realized, *Oh my God, you know what? I'm one of those energy sucker people!* I'd tell everyone my problems, leave, and feel so good. But you can bet they didn't feel better. I never saw it that way before.

I realized I needed to get over a few things. I needed to understand what happened, but there was still stuff I needed to learn if I was still begging for attention. *What have I learned from the accident other than how to get more attention?* You need to really look into your own heart in situations like this and figure out what's behind the way you act.

Things like this go back to childhood. If you're a little kid in a grocery store, stomping your feet, trying to get your mom to buy you a toy and instead, she smacks you, how you're acting is not going to work. But in that moment where the foot stomping doesn't work, everything changes. It's the same thing when you're older. If attention is fed, it's definitely going to want more, and it doesn't matter what kind of attention it is.

One of my teachings is very powerful. I call it the *Power of Resistance*. You can use this to quit smoking. You can use this for anything at all, really.

Here's how it works: When a thought comes into your mind, it's looking for something. It wants to connect to something. *What?* Attention. For starters, the thought wants attention, but *what's going on behind the attention?* There are feelings and emotions. So when the thought comes, you have to stop it at the door. Every time you entertain the thought or let it hang out with you, it drags you down. *What kind of friend is that?* You don't want to be hanging around with a thought like that. That thought might seem like your friend because you've had it a long time. You have to say, *Listen, we're not going there today. You wait right here, I'll be back, I'll be back. Just wait here on the doorstep.* But then you just leave the thought outside the door until it gets no attention and goes away.

There's another way resistance works on you. After my accident, when I was really mad about not recovering like I wanted to, I had a specialist doctor—a neurologist. I had to go down to the big city every month to see him. One day when I was in his office, he grabbed me by the shoulders during our appointment.

He gave me a little shake and said, "Stop trying to get back to where you were and accept where you are. You're not the same person you once were. You need to accept where you're at."

That hit me right between the eyes. I realized I was fighting so hard to get back to the way I was. I was letting thoughts through the door and was entertaining them. I had to leave them outside the door after that, until they went away.

RELATIONSHIPS

You have a relationship with your thoughts just like you have relationships with people. And if your thoughts are not really working for you, you need to change them. You have to look inside and take an honest look at your thoughts, how you're programming yourself or filtering information.

If you're in a relationship with someone and keep making excuses for it or asking yourself why you stay, you have to look at that. Most of us are willing to put up with a lot, what we're willing to accept as love, until we see things differently. You might have grown up with a family who fights and yells and screams and verbally abuses each other. So, you got used to it. That's how you think things are. As you grow and mature, your hurt gets a little more tender. You require the change that you've changed into. And if the other person hasn't made changes, you outgrow them. It doesn't mean you stopped loving them. It's a part of life. It's not right or wrong. It is what it is.

You might be in a relationship with alcohol. I get a lot of women who tell me:

Joseph, I drink too much wine.

Well, what's too much?

I start off when I'm cooking. I'll have a couple of drinks after work, you know, and then that bottle's gone. Sometimes it's two or three bottles. And I'll crank up the next night doing the same thing.

Okay, well if you're drinking two or three bottles, then you must have some cigarettes or a cigar too.

Joseph, how did you know that?

Because it's common sense. They go together, drinking and smoking. Does your sister know about this?

No, my God, no, they're church people!

Okay, here's what you're gonna do. You're gonna invite your sister over for some wine and cigars . . .

What? No! Why? Oh, no, no, no, no. She would judge me!

Here's the thing: Don't quit doing stuff that you love because you're setting yourself up for a battle. If you try to quit something you love, you're going to start fighting against it. You're acting like a kid with a new babysitter, seeing what you can get away with. But as soon as you admit what's going on in front of other people, it's not a secret. It's not fun anymore, and you have more control over it.

ADDICTION

Addictions—I've been through all that stuff. I've already tortured myself with that crap. That's how I learned the coolest thing. I realized addiction is a part of my greatest strength because I have an ability to commit. I've committed to things even if they weren't good for me. If I can commit to something that's not good for me, *what if I find something that is good?* The strength of commitment is already there. All I have to do is find it. Everything else is lined up.

I totally believe that every successful person in this world has got an addictive personality. I think Michael Jordan was addicted to bouncing that basketball. I think that he made a living and he honored that, and the next thing you know, he's the greatest in the whole wide world. I think there was an addiction in there. There's a craving inside. He wanted to play basketball. It was in there. And so that was an addiction, but he found an avenue to satisfy it. And in this case, the basketball addiction satisfied him. What a beautiful thing. So, I say people with addiction, they are powerhouses. Once you find something good to commit to, there's nothing in this world that can stop it. And it's already been proven through the addiction.

When you have an addiction, I always say it, honor it, get everything about it out of it. Learn everything you can from it because if you quit in the middle of your learning process, then there's a good chance you'll return to figure the rest of it. It won't fully be gone. So, the first thing when you're addicted is to acknowledge it. And I think that's why in AA everybody stands up and says, *I'm an alcoholic, my name is such and such.* There's something about that, about the acknowledgement of it. I always say learn everything you can in this moment because once you decide that you're going to make that change, you don't ever want to go back to learn what you need to know right now. Get it out of your system because change is coming.

How do we get ourselves to the point that we want to change? That's different because I think that has to do with self-love. The more I started loving myself, the less I wanted to escape this world.

When I was a drinking person, I'd get all bent out of shape and was ticked off at everybody. Mad at the world. My relationship went sour. Then, *blah, blah, blah, blah, blah,* I turned to the alcohol. I was drinking, and then I went through more turmoil with the drinking than I did with the problems that started the drinking. Then, the solution was to quit drinking and just face the music. *She's gone. You cannot force people to love you Joseph. That's it. It's over.*

I'm not a drinker now, but I appreciate every drop I ever drank. When it's time to give stuff up, it's sure nice to know everything about it. It's like when people say, *Keep your enemies close.* You know what I'm saying? With the booze and the addictions, it's very tricky because it's strong.

A lot depends on what you do with your story. If you went through twenty years of what you now see as abusing yourself, you've got to look at that and ask, How does that feel? Maybe you'll say, *It sucks man—all of those wasted years. What, are you gonna waste more time looking back at them?* You have an opportunity of a lifetime to help other people going through the same thing. You could go to University and not learn as much. Now on the other side of the so-called *wasted years,* it's like you're the professor. Get up, preach the message because you've been through it. Your words back up your life. Then, what happens is you're walking, living, and speaking your truth. And that's what everybody's hungry for, the truth. The truth is how you got through it. What a powerful message that is to talk about. *I went through that same situation as you did, and I got through it.*

OUTGROWING PEOPLE

If you're in a relationship and your partner is not where you're at in life, and you're not happy, you need to start doing things for yourself to bring in some joy and happiness. If you're growing in different directions, don't waste your time hating the other person. Go experience and live life. If someone doesn't want to go along, that's fine. You outgrow people in your life and people will outgrow you.

I've really looked at this a lot, the outgrowing people and loving people in my life. I've realized how important it is. *How many people have I loved, trying to force them to love me, only wanting them to love me in return?* It's that thing of throwing those love seeds out, hoping some of them would stick. I don't do that anymore. I plant my own seeds. I want to make sure that my love is honored and respected because when it is, then I'm going to share more love.

There's no sense in sharing all kinds of love with somebody, filling up their plate with so much that they can't even digest it. If I'm overloving and the love just sits there on the plate, it's just making a big mess. You have to think about what you're feeling in a relationship and ask the other person if they are feeling the same way. *Are you both the same number on the love thermometer?*

If there's something you want to work on, you can work on it together. If the other person is not in the same boat, then there's the answer; it's time to part ways. It's not easy though. Definitely the hardest thing in the world when you don't want to be with someone any more or they don't want to be with you. Still, loving somebody and telling them that you don't want to be with them is really hard. That's a devastating blow to a lot of areas in your life.

In my case, when this happened to me, there were a few things that I went through. I've been on both sides of this, so

I've managed to sift through a little bit more on the receiving end. On the receiving end, you have to build back up again because you're not feeling worthy.

After I met my wife and we got in our relationship, I could see some things happened to me. Now, when someone says to me, *I'm not sure if I'm with my soul mate, or my twin-flame,* I realize that if you were sure, you wouldn't have to ask. You would be saying, *This is my soulmate, my twin-flame.* You'd know it. I always had this thought in relationships, as beautiful as they were, there's got to be more. There's got to be something else. When I met my wife, I realized that thought disappeared. I wasn't having that thought, that there should be something more. Basically, everything in life—it's all how you see it and believe it to be.

If love is like a thermometer from one to twenty and you're an eighteen, it's really hard to share with a four. What you're constantly doing is waiting for them to catch up. Once they do, you've been waiting so long it's unbalanced and it's very, very difficult. It's definitely got to be a two-way street from the start.

When you go into a relationship thinking more in advance what you're getting into and what you're looking for, it's easier than wondering if there is more. *Am I happy? Do I need to part ways?* Those kinds of thoughts take a lot of energy.

Sometimes people go through a lot of abuse growing up. They end up getting into relationships where they are abused because it's all they really know. They never experienced anything different. So to them, someone yelling at them or abusing them, if that's the way they grew up, they accept it. That's love to them. Someone else will say, *Don't you dare talk to me like that.* That's self-love. When you start to realize that you're not getting treated the way you want, that's when you know you're outgrowing someone.

I believe that we have lots of soulmates. What that means is you're going to teach me what I have to offer in life. That's what a soulmate is. You're going to meet my soul. You're going to reveal everything in me.

People look for relationships and what they call a *twin-flame.* For me, that twin-flame is like two pieces of string. I've got my life. You've got your life. When we're together, we're encased in a wax of love, like a candle. The wax holds everything together, and at that moment, it's like we're one, but it's the flame that burns. We're two separate people together. Our flame is much greater together, and everybody can see it as well.

I also want to acknowledge that we're our own soulmates. When we fall in love with ourselves, then we really know what we have to offer in a relationship. That's the point where we say, I'm not going to settle for less than I'm willing to give. I want someone to meet me where I'm at. I don't want to have to change them. I want them to meet me at the same level of understanding of love and life as I do so we can grow together. I really don't want to go in and have to babysit. And today, that's a major concern in relationships. One of the partners feels like they're the auditor and the other one is not in the same program. That means they're at a crossroads; it's a difficult situation to face. If one person wants to grow and one person wants to sit idle, there are decisions to be made. Nevertheless, it's nice to know where you're at, even if it's a hard situation.

When you believe there is a soul mate, or a twin-flame, and you don't settle for less than you want, that's faith.

ISLAND FAITH

If you want to know your spirit guide, I'd ask, *Who's the first person you think of who has crossed over?* Then, you can make a list of the first ten people who pop into your consciousness. If those people *weren't* your spirit guides, they wouldn't even come to your mind.

My favorite ascended master is Jesus. He's the closest to me. He's not the only one, but he's there. Everything is really actually very simple. There are a lot of fancy courses out there, helping you figure stuff out. That's fine but you really don't need it. Here's how I see it. I'm in faith.

Imagine if you were six years old, on a big ship, and the ship went down. The waves might get you to the shore, a little island, with one suitcase that washed up with you. You'd have to survive; you'd have no choice. Maybe you'd find a cave and some bananas. The next thing you know, you'd be getting a little older. You'd discover a bird's nest and see some eggs hatching. When you saw those little chicks poking out of the eggs you'd realize there was a creator, something invisible, bigger than you. You might start communicating with that creator because you have no one else. And the invisible creator would talk back to you. All of your comfort would come from the creator.

Now, let's say you're an adult, and a ship finally comes along and saves you.

They'll drag you to the mainland, sit you down, educate you and correct your language. They'll tell you that everything you believe is wrong. All of your rituals and worships, everything is all wrong, wrong, wrong. It doesn't fit inside their box.

You just need to go back to that innocence and knowing, back to your island where you can communicate with your creator one-on-one. Back to innocence. My vision of life sometimes is to return back to the island. That's where I experienced all of my pain and learning and working through stuff on a daily basis. That's Island Faith. Everything that you're going to learn in life is on that island. And you learn it from yourself.

You get reprogrammed to get confirmation of what you know from someone else, but you don't need it.

ENTERTAIN GOODNESS

What do you think about? What thoughts do you entertain? It's up to us to entertain the good ones. The other ones, you can still learn from those. If I'm feeling a little anger or pain from something, there's still more stuff to work on, and I can dig a little deeper. It's only a feeling or an emotion. It doesn't have control over me. Or if does, then the emotion is asking for an extra look because it's like a gauge. If a person says something to me and I think, *Gosh, that's offensive,* those words left that person, floated across to me, and put a little cage around my heart. Then the door shuts. Now those words, whatever the words were, whether they were angry or abusive, whatever they were, they've got life in them. Those words have life in them, but now they're sitting in this cage and start poking at me with their little pitch fork.

Those trapped words are saying:

Hey, what are you doing? We don't belong to you. You don't own us. Who do you think you are, God? How come you're holding us hostage? Why don't you open up this cage and let us go? You're looking for forgiveness. You're looking for apologies. You can't get them. Open up the cage and let us go so we can get into our next life. We're angry words. When we come back, we're coming back as peaceful where it's the opposite, so please set us free. Stop holding us hostage.

When that little cage opens up, and you let those angry words out of yourself, I've realized something. When someone's in a fit of anger and yelling and screaming at you, it's because they trust you in that moment. They're being vulnerable. They're opening up. They're saying things they probably don't even mean, but in that moment, they're trusting you not to beat them up or hurt them. They're having a moment. They're letting it go. I've realized I'm going to let those words flow by. I'm not going to let them bend me out of shape.

If I lock up those words in a cage around my heart, they become pitchforks. I know that I'm going to go through the mill, and then other thoughts start to build. Now, I'll let those words go by and not take them in.

OLD WOUNDS

An older man came to see me once, he said:
Joseph, I hope you can help me.

What happened? Are you okay?

Joseph, it happened a long time ago.

Yeah. How long?

Grade three.

So, how old are you now?

Eighty-two.

Sir, that's a long time to be carrying something around.

Well, it's serious.

What happened?

I was waiting to go in line for school and the teacher didn't ring the bell yet. Johnny hit me from behind, got on top of me, and started beating me. He kept punching and punching. My lip was bleeding; my nose was bleeding. I looked up, and that's the day I realized I really don't have any friends.

Nobody here is helping me. My whole classroom, they all started chanting and stomping their feet, "Fight, fight, fight, fight," and the rest of the school came over. All of a sudden, I kicked him. I got Johnny in the mouth. I went to get up and he grabbed my pants. And when I jumped up, he pulled down. My pants came down and my dinky popped out. All the kids saw it, and all the girls were teasing me and laughing.

It was the worst day of my life after that. Later on in life, it was very hard to be sexual. That moment it really ruined me and so I want to kill him. I just want to kill him!

I said sir, "Please stop talking. I'm a feeler, and what I'm feeling now is a lot of anger, hate, and resentment."

I'm not done yet. There's more I should tell you!

Holy jumping, man. Let's just calm down. Stop talking please. Man, when I feel into your story and I feel Johnny, he's in a whole different situation.

What? Johnny? What the hell does he have to do with this?

Well, you came to me for help. I'm trying to help and when I feel into Johnny, I've got to ask you sir, were you the tallest kid in your classroom?

Yes, I was. How do you know that?

Because I know when Johnny came to school that day he wasn't looking for a fight, sir. How do you think a kid in grade three knows how to fight the biggest kid in the classroom, put them down with his fist? He was getting beat at home and when he pulled your pants off, his pants were coming off at home too, and it wasn't a pretty sight . . . just saying.

He stopped and was silent for a minute with his head down. "I didn't know that happened to him."

You'd better look at me now. I'm proud of you. You're healed.

What do you mean I'm healed?

You just changed the way you feel about Johnny. I heard it when I told you Johnny was being molested at home. Your breath came in, there was a sigh, and then you released it.

I didn't know that was happening to him.

In that moment, sir, you were healed. You've been thinking of Johnny your whole life. You were entitled to think that way. It happened. But now it's different. Once you've changed that feeling, everything is going to change. You're going to be okay.

I'm a feeler, and when I felt into the situation I could feel his pain, but I could also feel Johnny's pain. That's a part of my gift. That's why I say, *I love everybody*. I really do and I love to the core and nobody complains about that love, but they will complain if I take something personal to that core. I really don't have a choice; that is how I love. That's how I feel; I feel to the core. When I *felt* the story, I could feel Johnny's pain too. And that's actually what helped the man. So in that case, that wasn't a psychic reading, that was not spiritual. What that was was him, sitting down with me being a feeler, and telling him how I felt. That let him have feelings about what could change. As soon as he did, he was healed.

The future of healing is feeling.

That was a very strong example of someone reacting to a story, even though it happened a long time ago. There are also things that happen to us when we were three years old, and we don't remember them. Like putting your hand near the stove and your mom tells you you're going to burn yourself. You pull back, you're scared, and you think you've done something really terrible. Those things get buried within us, and the fear can return years later when something happens. You have to find your own answers when life is not working the way you want it to. Asking other people what they think is probably not going to get you the answer you need.

EXTERNAL AND INTERNAL FEELERS

There are external feelers and internal feelers. It's nice to be in the presence of someone who knows how you feel, but you can't put the expectation on other people to feel the same way you do. That's not the way it works. Some people are both internal and external feelers. Some people love to have massages and are huggers, and some people take things in personally without the external part. Everybody's unique and different but stop trying to get people to know how you feel. Some of us feel internally and others feel more externally, but both are perfect and beautiful. There's nothing missing from either one. The most ideal relationship for me is when you have an internal and an external feeler together.

If you're an internal feeler, you might be really pissed off, mad, and upset, and you don't know why. Maybe your day at work wasn't even bad but you're just ticked off. Someone at home asks, *What the hell's the matter with you?* Then you get into an argument, over nothing. *Where's that anger coming from?*

Some people can feel into other people who are in the room and absorb a lot of emotions. What they're feeling doesn't even belong to them.

External feelers are awesome because they're what I call the *truth tellers.* They'll just tell you the truth and are not going to baby your emotions. It's beautiful to have an internal and external feeler together. It's like how a battery has a positive and a negative side, and it needs both sides because they're equal. My wife is an external feeler and it's nice to have someone in my life that understands me being so sensitive, rather than telling me, *Stop being so sensitive.*

If you're walking around and you're not paying attention to your energy or your feelings, feeling whatever's around you, that's going to drain you. If I go to a shopping center and I'm not thinking about my energy, I'll come home and be drained. I'm using up all my energy feeling things. I call it *Walmart Syndrome.* No offense to Walmart, it's got nothing to do with Walmart. It's just to describe locations that have a lot of people and energy in them. Every possible emotion is in those places at the same time.

When you're really sensitive and an internal feeler, you're going to feel tired and fried in certain places. I try and protect myself a little bit ahead of time, but I'll be honest, there's not much I can do. If I'm going to Walmart, I'm going to be tired after I get out of there. I'll order online, stay away from or spend as little time as possible in places that drain me. Get in, get out, and don't hang out.

If I walk in a flower shop, I'm not going to get burned out. I'm going to feel loved, appreciated, honored, and respected. I'm going to feel tenderness. That's way different than Walmart. So, we have to be aware and cautious.

When I know that someone is an internal feeler or takes stuff to the core, to the heart space like me, then we're going to be communicating on that same level. That's a beautiful place for me to be.

ENERGIZED PRAYERS

I think about *manifesting as energizing my prayers*. Before I met my wife, I was making prayers to the Creator of this universe asking to be in love. I wanted to be in love. When I met my wife, she was the answer to my prayers. So I said, *Thank you*. I didn't take the credit for creating her. Her mom and dad were the ones who burst her into this world. I can't take credit for something I didn't do. I put it out there and my prayers were answered.

When you want something to happen, dwell on how you would feel when it does happen. Then, let it go. At that moment, it's released. It's out there.

When someone comes to me for a physical healing, it might seem like I healed them, but I'm not God. I can't say, *I healed them.* Something happened through me and it all worked out. If I was actually doing that healing, I would figure out how I could do it again and again and again. I would master it, and then I would go into all the hospitals with it.

I say *thank you* for everything I've received, the way people say thank you with a prayer before a meal. I don't take ownership for what God does. That's taking the driver's seat, but the reality is we're passengers. We get answers to our prayers and our faith energizes the prayers.

I take credit for doing my best and giving my all. I try to be the best person I can be. That's what I can credit to the results, the answered prayers. Those are the rewards and the blessings.

Even trash gives you the chance to say *thank you.* It's how you look at it. If I'm taking out the trash and the bag breaks, instead of cursing and swearing, I look at the garbage as wrapping paper of my blessings. And I say, *Thank you so much* for everything I have. Each footstep is an opportunity for me to say thank you until I'm finished.

Thank you. Thank you. Thank you. Thank you. Thank you. Thank you. Thank you.

Then the garbage bag goes into the can. *Is it trash or a blessing?* It all depends on the way you see it. It's a ceremony of thanksgiving rather than putting out the trash. I turn everything into a little ritual or ceremony. Everything, all day long, I set everything up to make sure that I'm going to enjoy it.

I totally believe the one we call Jesus was a ceremonialist. He did all kinds of little ceremonies and people called them *miracles*.

Was it really a miracle? I believe Jesus knew what he was doing in his experience of being a man.

There is a lot of stuff in the story of Jesus that doesn't make sense, and it's hard for me to understand. But when people talk about Jesus, they're talking about love, forgiveness, and trust. It's like Buddha representing enlightenment, same kind of thing. *What does Muhammad Ali represent?* Self-defense, protection. Put up your dukes. Everything and everyone represent something.

Manifesting for me is really about hope, as a whole. You can't take ownership of what God does. If something doesn't happen for me, then it's timing or just not meant to be. I'd rather say *thank you* for all the blessings that I've received than take credit for them. I can't force things to come to me.

FAITH

Faith is trust and belief; you're trusting and believing in something that you can't see. It's not physically there. If you build something with your own hands, like a garden, you created a physical situation, but God makes the plants grow.

For me, it's all about the offering. That's what everything boils down to. Everybody's asking for things constantly. If I was God and looked down at everyone, I'd see a lot of red lights. The green light people would be the ones saying *thank you*. The yellow lights, in between, not ready to receive.

One time my wife wanted me to ask for something and show her how I did it. I got a couple of crystals out of the crystal fields. I was going back home looking at them. All of a sudden Spirit start talking to me.

So, what are you doing with those crystals?

Well, I'm getting ready to ask you for something on behalf of my wife.

What are you gonna ask for?

Well, I'm not ready yet. I'm not done.

Then, what are you doing?

I'm getting everything set up. What's with the trick questions? You were with me. You know what's happening. What's going on?

Joseph, are you taking stuff from my back yard and bringing it into my front yard and pretending that it's yours? And then you're asking me for your stuff on top of it? You're acting like you made the crystals.

Oh my gosh, you're right! That's exactly what I'm doing—taking stuff that you created and then trying to give it back to you, yet in hopes it'll get favor, and asking for things on top of it. Oh my gosh, that's terrible. What's the matter with me?

Well, what's your offering, Joseph?

I don't have offerings. I can come to you with my love . . .

No, that comes from me. What else have you got?

My hair. I'm always cutting my hair. I take my hair out of the brush, cut it up in the spring, and let the birds take it to their nests. When the chick hatches and takes its first breath, it's like they know me. But you know all of this stuff.

I got to thinking about it. Here's what I did. I cut my fingernail off and I offered it. That's a part of me, it's made of protein, like my hair. After that, I started offering my finger-nails to plants in my garden to help them grow. That's a part of my DNA. And I'm the only one who can offer that unique gift.

What a lot of people would call *manifesting*, I call *motivating*. That's doing something about what you want. You don't sit around waiting; you do something about it. And I like to create some kind of ceremony with an offering. That's what I mean by *doing something*.

LONELINESS

Loneliness is a beautiful thing because it teaches us the opposite of our desires. When you go through what I call *the learning process of loneliness*, it doesn't necessarily mean that you're all alone. It just feels like you're alone. Even if you're in a relationship, you can feel it, you know? There's always something more to the picture. It goes a lot deeper. You might be looking at your life saying, *Gosh, I've got everything I need. Everything's perfect, but I just feel lonely. I don't feel appreciated or respected,* or whatever the case may be.

You've got to do something about it. I like to personalize things. If I'm feeling lonely, something's missing. *What is it? What's missing?* When I do my self-discovery, I try and pinpoint the problem and work on that one. Sometimes when I'm feeling lonely, it's because I'm missing my mom or I'm missing the way things were or I'm wishing things were different.

It's really hard. There's not one simple answer to the loneliness. It's something that's an experience like joy; you go through it. *What is it like to be happy? The opposite of what it was like to be lonely? When you got happy, where did the loneliness go?* It was always sitting right there looking for the friend it needed. *What do you need loneliness for?* To appreciate your happiness.

There's a flip side of the coin to everything. If a coin goes through the mint and it doesn't get stamped, it doesn't have any value. It's a collector item maybe, but it doesn't have any value.

Some of the stories you tell don't hold value. It's a single-sided story or viewpoint. When I hear a story, I already know there's another side to it. In order to establish the truth, I need to flip to the other side of that coin. There's a positive and negative side to everything in life. That's a big part of it, to find the other side and then choose. *Which one do you want?*

LOVING EVERYONE

Some lady asked me once, "How come you love everybody so much?"

I had to be honest with her—it's because I did some stupid things and was hated for them. I felt what it was like to be hated by somebody and to deserve the hate. And I'll tell you what, I didn't like that feeling at all. After I felt that way, I said, *I'm never going to feel this way again. I'm going to do my best to just to love everybody the best I can.* I certainly don't like the way it feels to be hated. And I decided I'm not going to hate.

And if I'm going to love people, it's not about listening to other people, telling them what to do, how to love, or that they should be loving differently. It's about loving in our own way and knowing and taking comfort in the way your love affects the people in your life. And they do know you love them. The way you show it might be a little on the unique side, but it's okay. It's your way. You have your own unique way and it's perfect for you. If someone's not feeling your love, it's actually them trying to push you to love them differently. It has nothing to do with you. You just have to stand your ground and love the way you do. You can't force someone to love you a certain way, and they can't force you to love them a certain way. There's no sense trying to change someone else.

SECTION 2

RELEASE PROCESSES AND CEREMONIES

LETTERS TO THE MOON AND BACK

The moon teaches us that there's nothing to fear in the darkness. Darkness needs light to be revealed and light needs darkness to be appreciated. The moon has no light of its own so the sun uses it to reflect its light. The same kind of thing goes on here on Earth, with humans. But we're not darkness, we're a part of creation. So, our own consciousness lights us like the sun lights the moon.

If you look at the moon when it starts out full, it's like your whole life. The next night, if you watch it something seems missing, even though it's still there. You can't see it. You can use the moon as a constant reminder of letting go or opening up and receiving. And it's such a beautiful thing.

For me, the moon is very personal. I get up very early, and I've been watching the cycles of the moon for a few years now, and it's been just fascinating to me. There's a lot more than meets the eye than just seeing the little slivers. There's a lot more to understand, to know about the different moons and the different seasons. People have been using the moon to bounce everything off of forever. I use it as a grounding or as a reflector.

If you start off when the moon is full, you can ask, *What am I full of? What could it be for me?*

I would start right away with *insecurities* because I figure if I can get rid of my insecurities, I've got a fighting chance.

So, the first night I would write a letter to insecurity.

Dear Insecurity,

I've had enough. You know, you're controlling and I can't do this anymore. Our relationship is changing. And now, you need to sit in the back seat. I'm driving now.

The next night, *pride,* the next night, *ego,* the next night, *jealousy,* and the next night and next night, something else. Through the cycles of the moon, I can release quite a bit. Now I'm empty and I don't even see myself. It's because I'm going through my new process. So when you're releasing to the moon, it's like you're outgrowing that part of yourself or you're outgrowing insecurity. But if it comes back, you can just do it over again another time and get rid of another layer.

Whether I'm mad, jealous, angry. It doesn't matter. It's still part of me. When I was building my house, I smashed my thumb with a hammer. I started yelling and screaming and swearing. My wife said, "Oh my God. I never thought I'd ever hear words like that coming out of you!"

I said "What? What do you think? You don't think I have the ability to get mad or angry or upset? You've just never seen it before." I said, "Well, just know this. It's there. It's very real. But don't get mad. Be happy that I've got that side of me, that I have the ability to get mad and angry. I'm a human being. It's part of me. Everybody's gifted to feel."

Every single thing to me is like setting up for something. When you're a little kid, you might be playing cowboys and Indians or army. You've got all these little men. Well, that's what it's like for me. Everything is one big setup, but I'm using nature and everything around me. Then, if I can pay close attention to what's going on, I've got a better chance to overcome what's ahead of me.

I look at it like I'm the teacher. If I let pride, ego, and jealousy hang out together at recess, they're going to cause a lot of trouble for the whole school. So, you know what? I need to separate them. Ego, get in the corner. Pride, you, over here. Insecurity, stand beside me. It's the only way I can get through to them when they gang up. I don't have a chance, so I need to separate parts of myself in order to understand who I am and what makes me *me*. I set it up like an army camp and that way I can understand myself. It's easier.

LOVE LETTERS TO YOURSELF

I wrote myself a really neat letter and was waiting for it to come in the mail. My wife caught me and asked what I was doing. I said, "Well, I've got a letter coming, and I didn't want you to see it."

Who's it from?

From you?

What? I didn't write you anything!

I know. I did it for you. I like doing stuff for people, you know?

I'm always out there helping people. 'Here, I'll get the door for you. Let me do this. Let me do that.' Well, I wrote this letter for you. So when it comes, you better go get a little whiff of your perfume from your cupboard.

When the letter came, I said, "Who's this from? Oh, it's addressed to me and it's from my wife." I opened it up. "Oh, my goodness, look at this:

To the most beautiful, loving Joseph.

You're the best cuddler, hugger, lover, stepfather, and father, my very best friend, and I love you."

It cost me less than a dollar to feel the things I needed to feel. I'm a man. I'm not going to burden my wife with an expectation that she'll write me a letter. I'm responsible to make myself feel the way I want to feel. None of my insecurities are real in her eyes. They're only in my own. They're my things to work on. They've got nothing to do with her. If I'm feeling inadequate, the only way I'm gonna know if she feels that way about me is if I ask her. It doesn't work that way. The best thing is to do is just do whatever it takes to feel the way I want to feel.

When I write a letter to myself, in that moment I do feel better. Some weeks I feel like I need to write a hundred letters. I do the same thing when I feel like I need an apology from somebody. There's no sense begging someone to apologize to you. They might not even know that they've done anything wrong, or they might not be consciously aware that your hurt and pain has gone deep.

If you write an apology to yourself, when it comes, receive it as an apology. You won't look at the situation the same again, and you'll be able to see beyond the problem. You do it for yourself.

There are things I need to work on, but I've got to do it myself. Writing myself letters of encouragement is awesome. I'm so excited to go to the mailbox. For some of the letters I might go six times before it comes, but every time I go, there's a great excitement and anticipation to get something or to receive, so every time I go to that mailbox I'm opening up to receive something. I can receive from myself and then start receiving from everybody else equally. That's huge, receiving from yourself.

Writing letters to yourself is a way to keep from constantly raking yourself over the coals in your head. You can't keep doing that. I love the fact that we're all teachers and students, and some people come into our lives and teach us exactly what we don't want— and some teachers teach us what we do want.

My feelings are a guide but I don't need to get wrapped up in the feeling. I just need to acknowledge what it is, honor it, and go with that. You can get caught up in your feelings. If you do, there's a good chance your feelings will catch up to your emotions. Once the two of those get together, I'm not saying you're in trouble, but it's got twice the strength and power in that moment. When you separate your feelings from your emotions and just use your feelings and notice how you're feeling about something, you're gonna set yourself free. You're going to understand how feelings are a gift. Emotions are a gift. Thoughts are thoughts, like words in Scrabble. They're just thrown out there and you have to use them to figure things out.

I came to this understanding in the past year. When I asked myself, *What do I think when I'm most likely to go wrong?* If I ask instead, *What do I feel?* then I don't go in the wrong direction. Feelings are a gift and the human mind, it's brilliant. It's crazy-awesome, and it can take us for rides. It took me years and years and years to master and to control my mind.

LETTING GO CEREMONY

The human mind is brilliant. If you use your mind to control or sidestep a few things, it can work to your advantage. I put triggers in my mind to trigger me. I have to see that a problem is gone. I write the problem or situation down as best as I can. Then, I sit outside and read it to myself.

I think carefully about what I'm saying, then I burn it. I put the ashes on the ground and then all the words in the letter are now in that ash. When a thought comes to me about that situation, I have somewhere to send it. I send the thought into the ashes. The ash becomes like the final thought, the final chapter. That's the period. You can save some ashes in a small vial and keep them near you. Look at the vial, give it a little shake, but you know that it's over.

That's a little letting go ceremony. Write it down, burn it, and release the pain. Send new thoughts that come right to the ashes.

Sometimes things that happened are really painful, un-forgivable really, and unfair. Bad things happen. With me, I know that I need to get rid of some old story I'm telling myself. If someone did you wrong, abused you, most of the time you can't go ask that person to say they're sorry. Maybe they've passed on, or they don't even know they did anything wrong. And sometimes, what happened is so painful, you don't even want them to know the amount of pain they caused. You might be afraid they won't care or they'll laugh. So, it's not worth it.

I know sometimes that I'm never going to get an apology from a person. So, I do it for them. I write a letter from them, read it, accept it, and realize that it's as close as I'm ever going to get to hearing it directly from them. It's not like we're going to be *buddy-buddy* again because I don't trust them after what's happened. But after that, I'm lighter. I got what I needed. Then I can burn it and send any thoughts I have about it right to the ashes.

When you see a person who hurt you, whether it's in your mind or in real life, see the problem as sitting on their shoulder and not inside of them anymore. Look past what happened. You're a human being too. *How many times have you been the person who hurt someone or said something offensive?* It's better to be loving and forgiving even if someone else isn't that way. *Why?* Forgiveness is something you do for yourself.

And if something that feels like it's unforgivable happened, forgive anyway because you probably had no control over it. Forgiveness comes from inside you. If you keep looking to other people for forgiveness, you're never going to get rid of anger.

THE PINECONE PROCESS

I wanted to share a story about how I learned about the different depths of love. It came to me early one morning when I was sitting outside. I like to watch the sun come up. As soon as the sun rose, I sat back with a red clay pipe I had bought from the Indian crafts store. I put some sage and sweetgrass, a little bit of seed in it, and grinded them together. As the sun peeked out and started to shine, I lit the pipe and a blew out the smoke across the light of the sun. Then I started my prayers. When it's real cold outside and you can see your breath in the air, for whatever reason, when you blend those three to-gether—the cold, the pipe smoke, and the sunrise—when you blow out the smoke, you can see all the colors of the rainbow in the smoke. The smoke drifts by and all the sudden it picks up the rainbow-colored lights. It's such a beautiful experience. A lot of times I'm sitting by myself, I'll look around and think, *Where is everybody? Everybody should be having a moment and experiencing this.* It's such a beautiful time of day.

When I was walking the dog afterwards, I went by a pine tree and noticed all the pine cones underneath it. They were all closed up tight because it just rained. The next day, all the pine cones were open. I said, *Hey, look at this. The pine cones are still alive, even though they've left their mom, the tree. They've still got life in them.* I took one of the pine cones and I soaked it in water overnight.

When you soak the pinecone overnight, it's going to close up completely. Then you put it out on a napkin or small cloth and look at the pine cone, like it's your heart or someone else's. Let's just say for example, I have a friend who's going through something. We'll call him Bill, and I already know, he's having a rough time, the soaked pine cone represents Bill's heart. Overnight it completely closed but that's okay because I'd rather him be closed up and start over. So, his heart is closed up. As the pinecone dries up, it opens up.

Then, I start at the tip and I said, *I love you. You're a good man. You're a good Dad.* Every stem that opens up, it's a level of love and I put a little blessing of love on it. Then, I decorate it and I make little Christmas ornament out of it for him. When I give it to him, I explain the story of what I did. I closed the problems up, reopened them and then started over. The decoration is a reminder of everything he's been through.

Even if you don't make a decoration out of the pinecone, you can still use it to say prayers. If someone you know or love is sick or going to pass, it's not easy to go through. There are two roads to take. One is to torment yourself and make yourself sick, worrying and suffering just like them. The other is to send them blessings and prayers from every layer of the pinecone.

I love you. Bless you. I love you. Bless you. I love you. Bless you.

I'm not saying the person is going to be healed. But the prayers are a better way to go through something than just worrying or feeling sad all the time.

I use pinecones for myself too, at home. If there's a pinecone on the table in the morning, closed up, it means somebody in the house is going through something. They're not asking to talk about it. What they're asking for is a little support from everybody in the house. When the pine cone goes on the table, we don't talk; we just send blessings. Everybody touches it as they go through their day, sending blessings. Once it's open, it's up to the person if they want to talk about it or not. What they were asking for was some support through their problem. A pine cone is a good way to communicate in silence, especially with a big family.

SHOE REMINDERS

Something I do that's really simple and works for a few different reasons is to put a reminder in my shoe. Every day, when I start my day, I like to have some story, some memory, a good memory. If I'm going through a tough time, then I want to keep repeating the good story throughout my day. I'll put a coin or a little pebble in one shoe, something I'm going to feel. As soon as I feel it, I use it as a trigger and I rehearse the good story in my mind. The story is always a happy one, so if I have a lot of happy thoughts going through my day, my day is going to go pretty well.

LIGHTEN YOUR HEART WITH A FEATHER

Another simple release ritual you can do is with a feather. When you're walking around, especially by a lake, look for feathers. Then, with a feather in your hand, the first thing you do is give thanks to the bird that dropped it. It came from nature and there's a lot of purpose in appreciating the feather.

Start to look at the feather a little closer. Imagine the stem as your heart. That's your center, your heart. Look at all the little fuzzy things that have gotten attached to your heart. Each tiny part of the feather is light, but together they add up. So, those things weighing down your heart need to go. It's like taking your heart in your hand. All of the little pieces go back to people, places, events, situations, memories, and then they braid themselves together like rope, causing you to feel like you can't move forward.

After that, burn the feather. As every little fuzzy attached to the center burns down, it's one of those things that you got attached to. It's getting released as it burns. You can feel the freedom but keep watching it burn. When a thought comes to you, that's a part of a story that you're letting go.

A ritual, even if it's a small one, is a reminder that you don't have to keep thinking the same way. You can create the rest of the story yourself and change the ending. You don't have to know what caused the problem, but you can change it to something that feels good.

GROWING SELF-LOVE

I decided I was going to start a patio garden and plant a few different things. I started thinking about it as a morning water ceremony. I went on my Facebook and asked if anybody wanted to put their name in the bucket. Anyone with any barriers or anything, someone on a bit of a rough road. When I watered, I'd send them blessings. I was watering anyway. I called it The Morning Ceremony of Loving Kindness.

I got almost 300 people. I put their initials on pieces of paper and put them into a thick plastic bucket next to a tiny tomato plant. I bolted the bucket to fence and I can't explain it, but at one point the wind ripped the bucket off and threw it on the ground. There was so much energy in it.

That one tomato plant produced more than anything else. It kept growing and growing like a bush! The idea was to say prayers for people who either needed forgiveness or for the people who needed forgiveness from them. Just sending blessings for whatever it was they needed.

Then, I got the idea to do blessings for people with names that had certain letters in them, like *zucchini*. Then, I stuck those names in a bucket and told them they're growing like crazy right now, like a zucchini. It's got big leaves that protect it from the sun and maybe a few other things you can't see while it's growing. So, I told them to just accept the fact that they needed to step back. Don't try to take center stage; become like the backup band. Just know it's not time for you to be out in the limelight right now. Sit back, take it easy, and grow. And when I put that out to those people, it really rang true for them.

Then I noticed one of the melons was caught in behind the fence, and I thought, oh, people with names like the letters in *melon . . . are you feeling trapped right now?*

Feel like you're not going anywhere? Feel like nothing's happening and you can't move forward? Well today, that changes because I took my nippers and I cut that fence and popped that melon out. I told them, now, after today, you're definitely going to start to grow. Sure enough, I saw that melon grow with my own eyes.

I was watching the garden but relating it to people lives. I did it from my Facebook page, but anyone can do it. It feels great to know that you've made someone's day, made them happy and gave them a little something to help carry them through their day.

The whole garden idea, it's all about self-love to me, and it's about feeling important and having a purpose even though you did it yourself. When you have everybody's names or initials in your little buckets, those people are counting on your prayers. Then, you become a source of love, respect, and energy in a way.

Maybe it's time to plant a garden and set up a morning ceremony to send blessings and prayers. I looked forward to that moment of watering and talking to all those people silently every day. It set me up to enjoy every moment of life all summer long. I was happy watering and sending away any bad feelings that had no importance to me or anyone else. It's a beautiful way to connect to everybody, and it's a good way to open up to receive. If you're pulling weeds and watering there's balance, giving and receiving.

You'll start naming those plants, talking to them, singing to them on good days. Those plants are growing from seeds. So when you say prayers and send positive thoughts, those things are growing inside of you. The plant shows you an example of what's happening inside you.

ANCESTRAL COIN SYSTEM

I created a simple but powerful system that can help you get accurate answers to everyday problems or relief from deeply buried wounds.

Get out a piece of paper and write down numbers from 1 to 9. Then, beside each number, write the name of somebody that has crossed over. It can be a loved one, someone you knew, a pet, a celebrity, anyone. Don't spend too much time thinking about it. Just go down the list and write the names as they come to you next to the numbers.

Let's say for example, the question of the day is that you're looking for a job and you've got a few different opportunities. You're not sure which one to take. When you go out and about on your day, look for coins on the ground. You'll find them at grocery stores, banks, and different places. Or look at the change you get when you pay cash for something.

Let's just say for an example, I find a penny. I look at the year and it's 1982.

1982

The first two numbers in 1982 (or any other year) get added together.

$$1+9 = 10$$

The sum of the first two numbers gets added to the third number.

$$10 + 8 = 18$$

The sum of the first three numbers gets added to the fourth number.

$$18 + 2 = 20$$

The final number is 20. Then, I separate those two numbers and add them to each other.

$$2 + 0 = 2$$

After that, I look at who number two is on my list. Then, I think about what that person or celebrity or pet, whoever, represents and get a message to help me with my question or decision.

If you need an answer right away, you can pull one out of a jar at home. Each coin represents a visit from an ancestor or someone who has crossed over.

Let's say the year on the coin is 1952.

1952

The first two numbers in 1952 (or any other year) get added together.

1+9 = 10

The sum of the first two numbers gets added to the third number.

10 + 5 = 15

The sum of the first three numbers gets added to the fourth number.

15 + 2 = 17

The final number is 17. Then, I separate those two numbers and add them to each other.

1 + 7 = 8

Who is number 8 on your list?

You can put the coin in the jar and thank the visitor from the other side. Once you start looking for coins, they'll show up. Over time, you'll realize how many visitors you get. If you're missing Grandma, you'll find a coin, look at the year, add it up, and be darned if it isn't Grandma. Now it's not that Grandma is actually in that coin. It's all done through connecting with your memory and feelings.

This is a personal way to get answers without having to ask anybody else. You don't have to ask anybody for anything. Your answer can be sitting at your feet, like a footnote.

When you're making your list, you ask yourself, *Who's the first person who comes to mind?* The first person is the one that's highest in your consciousness. It doesn't matter if it's not who you expect it to be. Just write it down.

What comes to mind when you think of the person?

What is the strongest memory of the person?

If you think of a story about them, what does that story mean to you?

Don't worry about what other people might think. Just go down the list and make notes about what came to mind about whoever crossed over.

Let's say you're deciding whether to take a vacation. Maybe someone on your list comes up that just sat in front of the TV and didn't do much. There's a message not to sit idle. Get out there and take that trip. Do something. Live your life.

As soon as you find a coin, you'll start to notice other signs and messages from the other side. It might be animals or birds or bugs. If you pay attention, you'll see them. There are a lot of answers you can get.

Let's say you're in an elevator, all dressed up. You might not want to bend over and pick up a penny in front of everyone. Put your foot over it, slide it toward you, drop something, and pick up the penny at the same time. It's all good. You don't have to be out there explaining everything to everybody. It's personal. Do things in silence and in Spirit.

Everybody has questions and is searching for answers. A lot of times it's not so easy to ask for help or guidance from the people in your life. Maybe you don't want to burden them with your problem or it's very personal. Sometimes it's not even fair to ask someone else because what you're figuring out is a part of your own journey. You need to figure it out yourself.

Using the coin system, you can always get help with your questions. It's nice and safe and you can connect with people who have already crossed over at home or wherever you are. Sit down and listen.

It's not like the people are coming from the other side and jumping back into this life into the coin. It's about connecting with the memories and lessons you learned from that person. Honor the feelings that you get. What you're connecting to with the coin comes right from your core.

NUMEROLOGY

I'm a total believer that you should follow your path and let your path change you. It's easier than trying to force changes and get into things that don't really suit you. I teach people how to follow their own path.

I have my own way of using numerology. I made it up; it works for me. You can use it for yourself, make something up, or use another numerology system. You don't need anything more complicated than just adding to use the Ancestral Coin System that I described in the previous section. So, don't complicate it by second-guessing yourself. The Ancestral Coin System is a simple and beautiful way to connect with loved ones who have crossed over.

This is something I like to do when I'm out in nature. I'm a counter and I like to count things.

Number 1 is a simple one, it represents me.

Number 2 is me and another person, or relationship.

Number 3 is Spirit.

Number 4 is the four directions on this earth—north, south, east, and west.

Number 5 is the four directions of the earth with me sitting in the center.

Number 6 is the four directions of this earth plus me and Spirit.

Number 7 is the four directions, plus me and another presence or person, one above, one below, perfectly centered.

Number 8 is, of course, infinity.

Number 9 is when everything starts adding up. If the number nine kicks in, it means things are starting to make sense: 9, 18, 27, 36, 45, 54, 63, 72, or 81. They all add up to nine.

SECTION 3

BLESSINGS FOR YOUR DAY

TRUE PURPOSE

I remember a wonderful clan mother telling me that I was too white to be an Indian and too Indian to be white. I was stuck somewhere in the middle to find myself. Her words ring loudly in my ears these days after discovering my true purpose in life was to follow and learn from "my own" shamanic thoughts and footsteps. All these years later, most of those thoughts have become beautiful teachings that I share with confidence, knowing firsthand that they work. Helping others heal themselves has become very natural to me over the years, and oh, how it satisfies and gives peace to my soul.

TWO RAVENS

It's amusing how Spirit has such simple ways of working within my human parameters of faith, trust, and surrender to get a message through to me. This past year, Spirit has been speaking to my heart, through two beautiful ravens that fly close by during spiritual land tours. One always does a nice, slow glide-by, not more than twenty feet away, with wings spread wide open with beauty and grace. The messages shared can't be denied, knowing how close she flies to capture my full attention in those perfect moments.

THE EIGHT BALL

Does anyone else remember being fascinated as a child, seeing one of those Magic 8 Balls, and wondering what it was? Once I found out it could tell the future, it got even more mysterious, but my mom said I was too young to try it. Amazing how your earliest fascinations in life can give clues of your career.

Turning your passion into a career comes easily once you discover the gifts that support them. I wonder how old Elvis was the first time he sang or when Tiger held his first golf club.

One of my gifts is seeing the gifts in others and then helping them grow into the gifts they are born with. If you're thinking of becoming a spiritual teacher/healer/shaman, then the first step is to put together your first session.

Every time you share your session with someone, you will learn from their experience and feedback. One step at a time. I remember starting with my first session and recognizing my own soul by doing it.

How wonderful life can be.

REACH FOR THE SKY BUT STAY GROUNDED

The Amitabha Stupa and Peace Park is one of my favorite places on earth. The tree carving of Buddha gives off amazing vibes of peace that flow through me like goosebumps. Amazing how strong and kind trees are, gifting us the air we breathe to stay alive and deep roots to learn from.

My tree friends here have taught me to reach for the sky while staying grounded and how to listen when nothing is being said.

Imagine being a tree and carved into a beautiful statue to represent something very special to so many people. The diameter of the carving makes me wonder if the tree was as old as the man carved into it. What great beauty and respect the caretakers here give to this beautiful land.

LET LIFE LIVE THROUGH YOU

Life can get exciting only if you let it.

Don't hold back on life, but let life live through you, accepting and dealing with one footstep at a time.

Make it a point to go easy on yourself this week and set in place a few things that you really will enjoy and look forward to doing.

Live within the joy that you're looking forward to enjoying.

LISTENING IS THE BEST MEDICINE

Healers, shamans, and teachers are all labels that people use to relate to others. A true healer is simply the person with two ears who knows how to use them. Listening is the best medicine a person can give another—then, offering advice from a sacred heart space of truth and love.

Labels, on the other hand, can be words used to describe the occupation or calling of a person's life that he or she is doing their best to follow.

Giving thanks this morning to all of you who have ears to listen and a calm heart to speak from, knowing that sacred space your holding.

THE FOUR-LEGGED SHAMAN

Healing and miracles are two different things. I take no credit for the few miracles that I have seen over the years. Those shaman footsteps may be my own, but when I study them, so many others have walked the same ones before me.

My greatest shamanic teacher of love left those footprints in the snow after barking at a rabbit and protecting the house like a good puppy does. If you want to learn about love, then get a puppy; if you want to heal, then take a walk into nature and simply let it all go.

SILENT NIGHT

If words could smell and hear, then I would write a note to be remembered by the silence this morning at 3:00 a.m. How wonderful to wake up to a very silent night covered with a blanket of pure white snow. Yesterday I was raking up the leaves and branches in the yard in a T-shirt under the warmth of the sun.

Message of the day is remembering how quickly things can change for the good in life, when I'm willing to do the work needed to get there.

THANKS MOM, FOR BEING YOU

February 3, 2008, was the day my mom stepped out of this life and into her next. Not a day has gone by without listening to the sound of her voice ringing through my ears. I believe she is now an angel, guiding over me from above. Her memory visits me though so many different things that one day, I realized that I was her sign too. Resting in peace is my mom, yet within every footstep taken, I can feel her walking within my shoes with me.

I love you "Mother Dear" more than ever, and simply am giving thanks for you birthing me into this life. Gosh, looking back, the first nine-months was when I listened to you from deep inside of you while communicating through a magical invisible connection. Now the roles have changed, and you still communicate with me as I grow and age into your lived-through wisdom left behind.

TAKE A PEEK THROUGH THE KEYHOLE

When I don't want to face the music, it becomes easier to just blame karma or a past life for the problem. The dang problem I found was that the song never stopped playing in the background until I discovered how to unplug it. Taking one tiny step deeper gives unseen answers to every footstep taken in both happy and sad days lived.

If my feelings and emotions get rattled, it's because they seek personal attention away from my peace. Now I use them as a doorbell and peek through the keyhole before answering or letting them in.

LISTEN TO THE CHILDREN

May perfect health and happiness fall upon us like full moon on clear night, making it easy for even darkness to see. There never really was anything to fear at night in the darkness, but it hovered over my bed like a cloud as a child. Every night I would wake in fear, feeling the presence of something invisible to the human eye but extremely *real* to me. Terrified, I just lay there frozen, too scared to move, but would peek through the crack of my eyes, pretending I was sleeping. Sweat would soak my blanket. I remember like it was yesterday, but at the time was too young to be able to explain it in words.

Those years of fear taught me what I teach today after having to figure out on my own how to overcome that sort of darkness. The cool thing is that now, when a parent calls, asking what's wrong with their child, I can comfortably explain how it's the child's gift to see beyond this world. If the gift is medicated or pushed away, then the child grows searching for their gifts rather than growing into them.

Let the children talk out loud, and then listen to what comes out of them, as if it was real, because in their little mind it is as real as it gets and filled with emotions. Memories stay alive because they end up teaching the other side of the story.

THE MAGICAL MOON

Constantly paying attention and remembering is basically one of the easiest ways of learning that I have found so far. Living under the time cycle of the moon has been my personal study for the past two years. By getting up every morning before 3:00 a.m., one of the first things I learned was how darkness holds space for light. Now I know that the moon is darkness, with no light of its own so the sun uses it to reflect its light. This moon cycle confirms that there is nothing to fear in the dark because it's a major part of creation to be learned from just the same. Moon tanning under this reflected light births something into my soul that can't be explained in words, but it's more like the feeling of a nice hug.

Good night and good morning from this interesting time in space.

LEARN FROM WITHIN

Life is the classroom outside of us that is studied from deep within. The teachers or guides are the feelings that surface during different subjects.

When feelings out-educate our understanding, there is no control over the emotions that can easily take us over. Those are the feelings used to measure the amount of willpower that has been accumulated through the battles of pain.

Feelings that are still stronger than the willingness to change are simply the things we're still going through in order to hopefully one day learn.

SIMPLE THINGS ARE IMPORTANT

Funny how desires change with age and how important the simplest things in life end up being as I get older. Mapping out our summer vacation. Traveling to visit family and friends up in Canada plus a few trees that I really miss sitting under.

Kinda kooky, but I am looking forward to listening to everyone talk while clearing the dishes after a big family meal. Rinsing dishes and composting the leftovers off the plates is like performing a baptism ceremony for me, and I really enjoy it.

The trash has become wrapping paper of my blessings and now a thanksgiving ceremony of footsteps from the house to the bin. Giving thanks this morning for traveling footsteps ahead.

SACRED PLACES

I don't take people to the popular main tourist vortex energy locations because I have found some more personal private power spots on my own. One of my favorite locations was shown to me by a very old native man who asked me to protect it before passing over.

He told me stories about the location having the oldest drawings around the area with very few locals knowing about it. He led us up a dry creek, telling me to step on the rocks leaving no signs that we were there. He cried when we got there, seeing human footprints left behind along with new drawings on the rock walls. Tears rolled down my cheeks, listening to him pour out his heart in prayer for the rocks to remain safe and unharmed.

My camera stayed in my pocket, feeling it too sacred to be taking photos and being alert, not to miss a thing or word spoken.

Great blessings to all the footsteps left behind since the families were living there over a thousand years ago.

SKEPTICS ARE THE BEST STUDENTS

The neat thing about my job is getting to meet so many different people from all over the world every day react to the beauty of Sedona. My favorite tours are the ones where wives sign up without telling their husbands that they're going for a spiritual experience. Gosh—there's nothing better than having folks of a skeptical nature come along for the tours because they are the type of people who never forget.

Skepticism works like a metal detector and triggers thoughts of disbelief to discover deeper truths that perhaps were never seen before. The key is being open to learn from the new things found that don't need proved to be understood.

WHAT MAKES YOU HAPPY?

The recipe to happiness was rediscovering what it is and not listening to what I was told it was. My concept of happiness has changed dramatically. Nowadays, even having a fly land on me makes me happy.

I remember my grade-seven shop class teacher always had cash money folded in his front pocket on display to draw attention. Like yesterday, I can hear him telling us that we have to get rich in order to be happy. Dang, we were one of the poorest families in the school so his words rubbed me the wrong way, thinking he was looking down at me. That uncomfortable feeling stayed with me for years so I studied it like a bug, learning everything that I possibly could from it, and now teach what I discovered through the process.

Happiness can be found in anything because it's a feeling that is different in every person and is measured like water fitting into anything that holds it. Big hugs to all of our teachers.

LET PAIN COMPENSATE YOU

A simple good morning smile and greeting from a stranger sure goes a long way with me, knowing how busy everyone is with life. I remember using things that happened to me in life as a big excuse not to change or move forward. Blaming the excuse was much easier than fighting through the pain of overcoming it, letting the anger convince others not to disagree.

"Step aside, pain—let's take a closer look at ya," is what happened one day, seeing my pain in a total opposite way. Looking back, I now understand how important it was to turn pain around and allow it to start compensating me rather than tormenting.

We will all go through whatever it is today to become who we will become tomorrow. So, what's really important is what we do with today.

Sending out big hugs and blessings within every smile shared and received today.

MOVING FORWARD

At times we drift along our path alone, until someone picks up the other paddle.

Gosh I love and trust my wife . . . trading both ends of the canoe with her knowing that together we don't drift but move swiftly forward.

FLAT LAND THINKING

Yesterday I had the most wonderful couple from California book a sunset tour, and during our conversation, a new phrase came out. We were talking about living in the past and the response that popped out of me in the moment was interesting. "Flat land thinking." The fella caught-on right away, so we had a good chuckle about how the Earth was thought to be flat by everyone at one time.

Flat land thinking was when I accepted things the way they were by innocently not knowing that there was more to be discovered. If the whole world could be wrong about something, then I could be wrong about a few things too. Speaking for myself, I can honestly say that many of my own personal views have changed over the past few years. These days, I find my soul wanting to catch up to the visions by sailing to the edge of discovery just to see what's there.

My world is no longer flat since my wife came into my life, using her natural gift of *woman's intuition* as a pendulum, linking our paths together. Gosh, every time she has one of her moments and I dive right in with full support, something cool happens. When a woman's intuition is followed, it also honors the spirit within her who sent it, and you never go wrong.

CALL SOMEONE TODAY

I can't get mad at people who never call me, but I am well capable of picking up the phone and calling them myself. Folks, don't wait around letting your mind get filled with excuses why not to call someone you're missing. Go with your heart and make the call you've been waiting for. Next thing you know they'll be saying, *Hey I was just thinking about you and was going to call.* Great minds think alike, they say, and I totally agree!

Great blessings to the "feelings of missing" and to Alexander Graham Bell for picking up the first phone and linking us all together as one. May today host communication, like clicking wine glasses together from thousands of miles away.

LIFELONG LEARNING

Loving that with years rolling by, the eagerness to understand what has already been learned has become more important than adventure. Discovering new ways of learning is simply a wonderful way to understand the journey of life.

May understanding become the icing on the cake of your adventures.

EVERYONE
HAS UNIQUE GIFTS

A wonderful healer came to see me the other day, just to recharge and clear during a spiritual land tour. Most clients who come to see me for energy clearing are those serving the public in one way or another. At times the different sorts of energy pile up within the memory bank or fills their heart space, causing other difficulties.

Like a train, we unhook the caboose from the engine to make it easier to clean out the boxcars, one at a time.

Some people are too busy to learn and would rather pay someone else to do it for them. Others come as healers to learn how to help those around them.

Interesting how some are gifted to walk into a room, feel the tension in the air after an argument or a fight took place, knowing nothing about anyone standing in the room. Those who feel these sorts of things are also those who find it very easy to learn about energy exchange and clearing. It's hard for them at times because they actually feel it all around them every single day.

Every person is born uniquely gifted within themselves in so many different wonderful ways to be discovered after slowly growing into themselves over time.

May we never stop learning new ways of learning.

SUNDAY IS SACRED

Sunday morning is the global day of gathering to worship in different faiths, yet only God understands the multiple creative ways of worship.

One thing for sure is that there are beautiful old ways of following God through religion, culture, or spirituality. It is amazing to have the blessing of so many people crossing my path from all over the world while doing spiritual land tours. Over the years, I learn more and more by having the opportunity to ask thousands of people a few simple questions.

Interesting thing is that most people these days crossing my path have taken bits and pieces of different belief systems and simply follow their own.

Within the tours, I share from what I learned the previous year or what has molded more change within each footstep taken. Giving thanks this morning for having such a beautiful classroom to learn, teach, worship, and grow in.

CHEERS, MOM!

I got all emotionally crazy inside yesterday missing my mom. So, I did a very different kind of ceremony to connect with her *her way.*

Mom asked me before she passed if, once in a while, I could bring a beer to her gravesite and just pour it on the ground for her. Well yesterday, I grabbed a can of beer that I had sitting around for over a year and stood still for a moment with it. Thinking of my mom, I cracked the tab of the can of beer open holding it up to the big blue sky and yelled out, "Cheers, Mom!"

Slowly I poured the beer into our compost bin, doing a ceremony of tender loving kindness for all the happy and sad memories that rest within me of my mom. As I looked up to the sky after closing the lid, there was a cloud shaped like a memory of her gifting me the feeling of her hugging me. She shows up in so many different ways every single day, just to let me know that she is with and loves me.

Missing my mom, yet always finding new ways of letting her know how much she is loved and remembered daily.

LISTEN TO THE WIND

May your day be filled with blessings of love through the hugs within the winds today from our beautiful Mother Earth.

LET LIFE LIVE THROUGH YOU

I just accept myself the way I am and go from there, following my path and letting my path change me.

So many things in life don't really need to be healed, but simply seen in a different light or way, transforming them into learning experiences and teachings.

Forcing change can put a detour on your path, taking longer to understand the messages from each of the road signs.

Go easy on change this year by following your path one footstep at a time (nice~n~slow) not to miss a thing.

THE OCEAN

The smell and sound of the ocean is a meditation all of its own, with no instructions needed to enter the door of nature's peace and beauty. Footsteps left behind in the sand for only the moment between each wave, with the ocean breathing in and out water rather than air. The ocean is alive and one of the most powerful teachers of how important it is to go with the flow and ride the waves.

INSIDE, YOU'RE STILL AN INNOCENT CHILD

Everything done as a child is automatically upgraded while growing into adulthood, making it easier to learn from the past while still being that child.

PLAN THINGS TO LOOK FORWARD TO

Spiritually speaking, one way of being present is by planning a few things out to be enjoyed and appreciated in the future. Allowing the excitement to build while waiting for them to happen is simply just good medicine for the soul's digestive system. By the time this set-up moment arrives, with all the waiting will come a very deep interesting unique feeling or relief to be remembered.

Next future set-up for me to be enjoyed is to have a cup of coffee with a good friend.

BE HONEST WITH YOURSELF

Teaching through living example is all about being honest with feelings and emotions rather than fighting against them with my pride and ego. Every answer to a problem stands back to back with you, waiting for you to turn around and face it.

If you stir jealousy into the mix, it can cause anger to overpower your feelings and emotions, causing your temper to pop the lid. All this is basically from not knowing how to simply ask for a little well-deserved attention.

Temper tantrums demand attention but the satisfaction is coming from insecurity and lack of self-control. The attention is stronger than willpower and feeds addiction. Then, you might search for an escape vehicle to medicate, rather than mediate, the problem away.

All this stuff that I teach is simply the self-discovery of the things I've had to overcome and learn from, explaining the simplicity.

ONE GOOD THOUGHT AT A TIME

Happy are those who think healthy thoughts on purpose to simply protect their mind from negative ones getting in, knowing that we can only entertain one thought at a time.

For years I have been teaching what I call *power of resistance* through thought replacement, and it's been working awesome for people. This process helps people obtain a little control of their mind and wandering thoughts to recognize *thinking patterns* that might need attention or tweaking.

Like a teacher in the classroom, I am very proud of my students who have gone on to teach the lessons I taught them and were able to witness healing in the minds of so many. I learned so much when I had no control of my own thoughts in the days of blaming others for getting in the way of how I wanted to feel. Also recognizing that the depth of the pain people are in is a calling to help others going through the same thing and heal.

To be honest, my teachings are very simple and easy to follow because they came to me in such a simple natural way. Like a peaceful warrior, during sessions we simply go through the battle plan to end up on the top of the mountain.

Write down three happy, healthy thoughts this morning, and put a nickel in your shoe. Every time you feel the nickel, use it as a trigger to remember and the happy thoughts. The more often you feed your mind good thoughts, the more hungry it gets to entertain more. Just saying, because it sure worked for me with my mind now being the butler and me the backseat driver, still in control of the ride.

BE OPEN TO LEARNING

It's interesting how the laws of creation bless us with difficult things in life. Yet they're restricted by our willingness to learn from them. Being open to learn at the cost of being wrong is when the soul is ready to grow into wisdom. Peace of mind indicates that learning is done when knowledge is no longer arguing with wisdom.

CONCLUSION

I hope that this book was helpful to you and made you look at some things in your life in a different way than before. That's the key to getting over bad stuff that happens. When you look at your problems from a different perspective, they look different. All of a sudden, you can see a solution, even when you have been carrying pain or sadness around with you for a long time.

Getting this book out has been a lifelong dream for me. It's something I never thought I could accomplish but here it is. Now, it's an amazing feeling to know that the things that I've learned in life can get passed down to my grandchildren and younger generations. My wife, Leanne, is really to thank for making the book happen for me. There's a great lesson to surround yourself with people who support you and believe in your dreams.

SHAMASTE

LET'S CONNECT

Folks, if life has become too much to handle, and you just need a break, please consider a personalized, custom retreat with us. Amazing West Sedona views of Thunder Mountain awaits you.

If you plan to visit Sedona and want to book a Spiritual Land Tour or retreat you can contact me on my website.

josephwhitewolf.net

Customized individual, couples, and group retreats are available with accommodations included.

I also offer phone sessions if you're not traveling any time soon.

Facebook
Joseph White Wolf Sedona

YouTube
Joseph White Wolf - Through My Eyes

ABOUT THE AUTHOR

Joseph White Wolf was born with a natural spiritual gift. Spending most of his time in rural nature as a child, living off the land, Joseph's teachers were the animals and plants around him. He has never read a book and sources his teachings directly from nature and Spirit. His messages are simple and practical—relatable to everyday life.

His unique perspective has helped him create a client list that includes professional athletes, world-class stage speakers, CEOs, teachers, healers, and people deepening their spiritual paths.

Joseph lives in Sedona, Arizona, where he leads customized group and individual spiritual land tours and retreats.

Manufactured by Amazon.ca
Bolton, ON

25750070R00074